ON TIME
AND METHOD

Applied Social Research Methods Series
Volume 13

Applied Social Research Methods Series

Series Editor:
LEONARD BICKMAN, Peabody College, Vanderbilt University
Series Associate Editor:
DEBRA ROG, National Institute of Mental Health

This series is designed to provide students and practicing professionals in the social sciences with relatively inexpensive softcover textbooks describing the major methods used in applied social research. Each text introduces the reader to the state of the art of that particular method and follows step-by-step procedures in its explanation. Each author describes the theory underlying the method to help the student understand the reasons for undertaking certain tasks. Current research is used to support the author's approach. Examples of utilization in a variety of applied fields, as well as sample exercises, are included in the books to aid in classroom use.

Volumes in this series:

ON TIME
AND METHOD

Janice R. Kelly
Joseph E. McGrath

Applied Social Research Methods Series
Volume 13

SAGE PUBLICATIONS
The Publishers of Professional Social Science
Newbury Park   Beverly Hills   London   New Delhi

For information address:

SAGE Publications, Inc.
2111 West Hillcrest Drive
Newbury Park, California 91320

SAGE Publications Inc.   SAGE Publications Ltd.
275 South Beverly Drive   28 Banner Street
Beverly Hills   London EC1Y 8QE
California 90212   England

SAGE PUBLICATIONS India Pvt. Ltd.
M-32 Market
Greater Kailash I
New Delhi 110 048 India

Printed in the United States of America

Library of Congress Cataloging-in-Publication Data

Kelly, Janice R.
   On time and method / Janice R. Kelly, Joseph E. McGrath.
     p.   cm.—(Applied social research methods ; v. 13)
   Bibliography: p.
   Includes index.
   ISBN 0-8039-3046-1   ISBN 0-8039-3047-X (pbk.)
   1. Social sciences—Research. I. McGrath, Joseph Edward, 1927-
II. Title.   III. Series: Applied social research methods series ;
v. 13.
H62.K415   1988
300'.72—dc19   87-32936
                               CIP

FIRST PRINTING 1988

CONTENTS

PREFACE

In the preface of our previous coauthored book, we said that we were thrice privileged—to be able to work on a topic (time) that is both fun and important in our field, and to do so in a supportive environment with help and encouragement from many people. This book grows out of that earlier book, and our work on it was aided by those same beneficial circumstances. We are even more fascinated by the topic. Its importance in our field is even more clearly established. And we have benefited from even more generous support, formal and informal, by the colleagues and institutions with whom we are connected.

This book has benefited from all the sources we noted in that previous work, and some others. One is the Social and Development Psychology Program of the National Science Foundation, which has provided support for a research program on temporal factors in group process and performance (NSF grants BNS 85-06805 and BNS 87-05151) with which we both have been associated during the period of development of the material in this book. We appreciate that support, which afforded us a chance to focus our scholarly efforts on a broad range of temporal issues, including some of the methodological issues dealt with in this book. We also appreciate the support, formal and informal, that we received from the Psychology Department and the University Research Board of the University of Illinois, Urbana, and from many colleagues in those organizations.

At the outset of this project, we were encouraged by Irwin Altman and J. Richard Hackman to develop this material. Gail Futoran and David Harrison, as colleagues on the time research project, helped us to develop and clarify our thinking. Len Bickman and Debra Rog, coeditors of this series, provided useful critiques and helpful comments on an earlier draft of the manuscript. Finally, we want to give special and emphatic thanks to Professor Donald W. Fiske, who provided a detailed review and critique of an earlier draft, and in the process both encouraged us to continue our intellectual struggles with this material and helped us to improve the material immeasurably.

To do research on time is a privilege and opportunity. To spend our scholarly efforts dealing with time and method is an intellectual treat. To do so with the support and encouragement of our colleagues is an honor and an advantage. To do so in collaboration with a valued colleague is a joy, indeed.

Janice R. Kelly
Joseph E. McGrath

1

Time and the Logic of Method

We begin with an apocryphal conversation, allegedly overheard while eavesdropping on a work session in a social and behavioral science research laboratory. The meeting was between S (student, subordinate) and M (mentor, master) about an experiment they were about to conduct. It could be prototypical:

S: I have to make sure I don't measure my dependent variable until after the experimental treatment has had time to take effect. Right?

M: Right.

S: Well, how long should I wait?

M: About 10 minutes?

S: 10 minutes? Why?

M: You have to make sure it has time to "take."

S: Will 10 minutes be enough?

M: I think so. That's how long Brown and Jones waited in their studies.

S: Why did they pick that time?

M: Why not? Besides, that's about all the time you can give to it. You have to leave time for instructions, and for task performance, and then for the questionnaires. So you probably can't waste any more than 10 minutes anyhow. Besides, if you waited longer, the treatment might wear off or something else might distract them.

S: But didn't Brown and Jones have some theoretical reason for 10 minutes?

M: Probably not. They already had too much detail in their theory, anyhow.

S: They sure did. They put all kinds of detail into it. Stuff about all the conditions and features of the experimental treatment—how big to make the stimulus cards, what color they should be, the exact order of stimuli, the exact words for the instructions, what level of language skill the S's need to have for the theory to apply, about the lighting in the room. All sorts of trivial details.

M: Of course they do. They are good scientists. You call them trivial details. But you need to control all those things to have a good, precise, quantitative study. So you can say with confidence, in your conclusions, that X caused Y.

S: Well, then, why didn't they have something in the theory about the time it takes for X to effect Y? And why don't we?

M: Oh, come on now! Everybody knows that time is not a theoretically interesting variable.

Much of our research methodology involves temporal factors, and our studies are vulnerable to many problems stemming from those temporal issues. A host of temporal factors—such as the temporal ordering of treatments and observations within a study, and the duration of the intervals between these events—are crucial to the conduct of our studies and to the conclusions we can draw from them. Yet, most social and behavioral scientists pay little attention to the temporal factors involved in their research.

The main aim of this book is to make explicit some of the important temporal features that are implicit in our research methodology, and to discuss how knowledge of and attention to those temporal factors can strengthen our research practice. In the first three chapters of the book, we will discuss temporal factors at each of several levels. We will start with the most macro level, discussing those temporal factors that are inherent in causal inference, such as a known time order, with the cause preceding the effect, and the temporal assumptions that we make about those causal processes when we map them to particular treatment-measurement intervals. Next, we discuss temporal factors that are involved in choosing and constructing research strategies and research designs, such as the degree to which different strategies allow causal processes to unfold in natural versus accelerated time and the ways temporal factors affect threats to the validity of study conclusions. We then move down to a more micro level, to discuss temporal factors in measurement and manipulation of variables. In the second half of the book (the final two chapters), we discuss techniques that can help deal with some of those temporal issues in research. Many of these temporal issues will be illustrated with examples drawn from our own discipline, social psychology. But we believe that the message applies more generally, to research in psychology and in a broad range of other social and behavioral science fields.

SOME TEMPORAL FACTORS IN METHODOLOGY

To get an idea of the many ways that time enters into ordinary research practice, think for a moment about the conduct of an experiment. We make **measurements** of **dependent variables** after some treatment or manipulation has been imposed on **independent variables** (or sometimes both before and after the treatment). This temporal ordering of treatment and effect is central to how we draw **causal inferences** about phenomena (i.e., the cause must precede the effect). (Terms in boldface type are defined in the Glossary.)

There are also many other temporal factors within our study procedures. We may have our participants perform a task for 15 minutes. We may deliver stimuli to participants at a **rate** of one slide per eight seconds. We may **counterbalance** the **temporal order** in which two sets of questions are answered. We may measure how quickly a participant responds to a signal. Or we may wait for a week before we measure the impact of a persuasive message on the attitudes of a group of study participants.

All of these temporal factors carry with them certain assumptions about or implications for the processes we are studying. But we may not always be aware of these assumptions. For instance, when we use **reaction time** as a measure of cognitive organization, we are assuming that a faster reaction time means that a piece of information is more accessible in memory. But this carries with it an additional assumption that there is a **linear** correspondence between space and time (i.e., a longer time to respond means that the information is farther away in memory), as well as the assumption that there is a linear correspondence between the process we are studying and time on the clock (i.e., that the way we reckon time psychologically matches the way time is represented on the culture's clock).

As another example: If we use a one-week delay before measuring the effects of some treatment, then we are making the assumption that a one-week interval is the amount of time necessary and sufficient for the unfolding of the causal processes that have been set in motion by the treatment. That is, we are assuming that, after a week, the full effects of the treatment will be felt, and will not yet have begun to fade. We are also assuming (or at least hoping) that very few intervening effects will occur within this one-week period (other than the effects of the treatment we want to study) that could enhance or inhibit the expected effect.

In many behavioral studies, we make only a single measurement of the process under consideration. A hidden temporal assumption here is that the shape of the underlying process is linear, or at least **monotonic**. If the process were **nonmonotonic—cyclic**, for instance—a single measurement would not be sufficient to capture its shape. In fact, the investigator can learn little about the shape of any process from a single measurement. Any single measurement could fall at the peak, or at the trough, or at the mean of the cycle.

We can make these points more clearly by describing how such temporal issues and assumptions are manifested in each of three areas of social psychology—social cognition, attitude change, and social change.

Social Cognition

Many of the time-based techniques used in experimental psychology are being applied in social psychology to the study of social memory and information processing. Use of these procedures requires a panel of strong assumptions about how temporal factors map within cognitive structures and processes. In this work, for example, reaction times or **response latencies** are taken to be indicators of any or all of three different sets of conditions or processes involving various research approaches:

(a) indicators of stimulus difficulty,
(b) indicators of layers or distances within internal cognitive structures, and
(c) evidences of performance effectiveness (i.e., speed of task completion).

Use of these time-based response measures rests on some further assumptions. First of all, use of these response measures assumes that all processes take some finite time—an assumption shared with the general positivistic approach to science, about which we will have more to say later in this chapter. Second, researchers who use response time measures must take some stand (at least implicitly) on whether the cognitive processes being explored operate in series (one after the other) or in parallel (two or more processes occur at the same time). Either way, they must in turn make some assumptions about how the amount of time needed for processing is affected by the (serial or parallel) form of the processing. Third, use of response time measures assumes that changes in the relevant behavioral processes map monotonically, and indeed strictly linearly, to important differences in cognitive organization. Fourth, such response time measures often involve differences in the millisecond range; and use of such measures assumes that time differences in that range are of consequence in regard to cognitive structure and processing. Fifth, such work assumes that all cognitive processes or subprocesses are always carried out in the minimum possible time—else why would quicker mean structurally or organizationally closer? Finally, this work ultimately implies that the measures involved (time to recall or recognize) reflect behavior processes that ultimately can somehow be mapped to the time course of various neurological processes as reflected in the brain. Together, those represent a heavy burden of assumptions, usually implicit, underlying the use of response time measures in research on cognitive structure and process.

In sharp contrast to these theoretically important but often implicit temporal assumptions that underlie the use of quantitatively precise response time measures, social cognition researchers make use of time concepts in a much cruder fashion in other aspects of their research. When they study such questions as how delays affect the recall of cognitive material, and how such delays alter memory after **priming** has taken place, there is virtually no specification regarding how long it takes for such processes to work. Delay intervals seem to be set far more on the basis of experimental convenience than on the basis of any attempt to reckon with the temporal parameters of the processes under study. The post delay measurement is likely to be carried out (a) toward the end of the same experimental hour, (b) at the same hour the next day or two days hence, or (c) at the same day and hour one week later. These time intervals seem to reflect class schedule patterns and other aspects of administrative convenience much more than they represent either empirically or theoretically derived temporal intervals thought to underlie the processes being studied.

Attitude Change

Such cavalier treatment of time intervals is also true in the attitude change area. Attitudes are usually defined as relatively stable patterns of beliefs, feelings, or intentions. Yet, laboratory studies of attitude change often seem to be based on the expectation that attitudes can be changed within the experimental hour or, if not by then, perhaps by the same time tomorrow or the same time next week.

Field studies of attitude change, on the other hand, are much more likely to deal with relatively long intervals—months, years, or even decades. As most researchers of behavioral science know, the longer the interval, the more the change in attitude may be reflecting other things (**confounding** events) rather than the events of interest to the study. Such studies may show no change when real change has indeed taken place, but faded or been counteracted by other **system** forces in the interim. Such studies may also show change when none that could be attributed to the variables of interest has taken place—reflecting such factors as **regression to the mean** and other confounding factors, as well as **measurement error**. Conversely, the shorter the interval, the more likely the observed change may reflect only the reactivity effects of the research operations themselves. Yet remarkably few studies of attitude change report any follow-up measures that could assess how long the putative changes persisted. These points will be examined later.

Social Change

Social change is always a very special methodological problem for social psychology. On the one hand, social change is part of the natural substantive concerns of the field. Measuring social change, however, is difficult. Change always appears in a form confounded with unreliability of the measures by which it is assessed.

On the other hand, social change has also been taken as an indication of the failure of social psychology to establish lawful relations, rather than being taken as a phenomenon to be regarded properly as a part of the field. In fact, some scholars (e.g., Gergen, 1973) have argued that, because our subjects of study (people) learn and change, social psychology can be at best only a systematic description of people at various points in history. This, of course, assumes that any lawful relation must be eternal or invariant over time. That our field should work on the assumption that only time-invariant relations are worthy of scientific study is strong testimony, indeed, as to just how little attention we have given to consideration of the temporal features of our field. Throughout this book, we will argue the contrary position, that *most* social psychological phenomena do not exhibit constancy over time, but show patterned variations or oscillations, regularities under specific conditions that themselves are a legitimate focus of our efforts to understand social change.

TIME AND CAUSE

Cause is a very complex idea. Discourse about it has filled many pages of philosophy books for centuries. Over two millennia ago, Aristotle set the framework for much later thinking on this topic when he defined four facets of the idea of cause: material cause (what the thing is made of); formal cause (the shape or structure of the thing); efficient or moving cause (the agent—person or condition—producing the thing); and final cause (the purpose for which the thing is produced) (Lloyd, 1968). Of these, it is Aristotle's idea of efficient cause that has dominated science, including social and behavioral science, since the time of Bacon, Hume, and Mills.

This idea of efficient cause presents a fairly mechanistic view of things. Such mechanistic causal chains, along with the **positivistic** philosophy of science in which they are embedded, have been called into question by much recent work in the philosophy of science, and by some researchers in the social and behavioral sciences as well (e.g., Gergen, 1985; Manicas & Secord, 1983). Some of those critiques have proposed philosophies for social and behavioral science that place one or another of the other three Aristotelian facets of cause—material, formal, and final—in the key explanatory role that efficient cause has occupied in our positivistic work. Manicas and Secord (1983), for example, propose as a substitute for positivism a neorealism that stresses an idea of cause similar to Aristotle's formal cause. And much of the impetus of the cognitive revolution in psychology derives from its frank teleological bent, which emphasizes goals, plans, and expectations as key influences on human behavior. These are all related to Aristotle's facet of final cause.

In part, these critiques of positivism have been prompted by the failure of research done under that philosophy to treat temporal matters adequately—as we will argue throughout this book. But the critiques of positivism extend far beyond those temporal issues, and to pursue those critiques in detail here would take us far beyond the scope of this book. Furthermore, a very large proportion of current social and behavioral science is still implicitly or explicitly based, philosophically, on some variant of logical positivism, and emphasizes only the Aristotelian efficient-cause facet in its causal inference structure. Therefore, in this book we will assume: (a) that we are concerned with social and behavioral science based on some version of logical positivism; and (b) that the concept of cause relevant to that science is based on Aristotle's efficient cause.

Aristotle's idea of efficient cause, as transformed through the thinking of Francis Bacon, Hume, and other philosophers of the enlightenment, is both fundamental to modern day social and behavioral science and shot through with temporal features. One can define the purpose of scientific study as the attempt to make causal inferences. We want to explain the **phenomena** we study. We want to know what caused those events, and what further events they will cause. Within our current **positivistic paradigm**, such causal inferences are essential to prediction and control; and, for positivism, prediction and control is explanation.

The temporal requirements embedded in the Baconian/Humean view of efficient cause can be summed up in three general propositions. If we think of X as the causal event, Y as the effect of interest, and the process by which X affects Y as the **causal process**, these temporal requirements can be stated as follows:

Cause must precede effect in time. Expected effect Y must come after putative cause X, thus creating both an X-Y order and an **X-Y interval.**

All causal processes take some finite amount of time. The time from X to Y (that is, the **duration** of the X-Y interval) must be long enough for the operation of the causal process by which X affects Y.

There can be no action at a temporal distance. The time between X and Y must be filled by the causal process.

In addition to those three temporal requirements of the Baconian/ Humean idea of cause, there is another temporal feature that operates not as a requirement but as a cue to causality: *Temporal and spatial contiguity.* The closer X and Y are in time (and space), hence the smaller the X-Y interval, the more likely it is that X (could be) a cause of Y.

Hume identified **temporal contiguity** as a kind of fool's gold of the causal domain: He argued that time order and contiguity are the only rational bases for making strong causal inferences inductively, but, nevertheless, they do not provide logically sound bases for doing so. The evidence is strong, nonetheless (e.g., see Einhorn & Hogarth, 1986) that people rely heavily on contiguity when they make judgments of probable cause. The same reliance is often a part of the scientific reasoning of our field.

The three temporal requirements of causality, and the crucial cue to causality, temporal contiguity, are discussed in the rest of this section of the chapter.

Time Order and Causal Interpretation

Temporal relations are at the very heart of our causal inferences. According to the logic of causal interpretation that has dominated our science (and our culture) since Hume, there must be a known time ordering between two events before one of them can be posited as a potential cause of the other. If event B follows event A in time, we know that event A may be the cause of B, and we know even more surely that event B cannot be the cause of A. Such a known time ordering, in which cause precedes effect in time, is at the heart of our causal reasoning.

We have developed our experimental designs and procedures around this temporal ordering. To explore a causal relation between two variables, we manipulate one, and then, after a period of time, we measure the effects of that manipulation on the other. Insofar as we can rule out the operation of other causal factors, we can become reasonably sure that the effects observed on the second variable are (or may be) a result of our imposed changes on the first.

This logic specifies that our chain of causal reasoning must move forward in time—a cause cannot follow an effect in time. For time to run backwards, or for the relation between effects and causes to run backwards in time, is forbidden in the current conceptions of time of our culture (and in the current conceptions of time in the methodology of our fields). This is not the case for all possible abstract conceptions of time, such as those that underlie the classical eastern philosophies. (See McGrath & Kelly, 1986). But in current social science, if causal time were to run backwards, our whole edifice of causal interpretation would collapse.

Alternative ways of conceptualizing cause and effect have been suggested. For instance, an ahistorical or systems view of causality does not specify particular events as being the causes of subsequent events (See glossary for **ahistorical causality**). Rather, under this view, a number of systemic forces operate simultaneously and in a mutually interdependent fashion to cause the extant system state. All of these forces together constitute a kind of system equilibrium. Change is manifested as a disturbance in one or more of the systemic forces that causes changes in other forces, more or less simultaneously, until the system is reestablished at a new form of system equilibrium.

This alternative to the Humean time order as the basis of cause/effect relations also gives a very central place to temporal factors. The system position does not permit time to run backwards any more than does the standard positivistic causal position. It simply downplays the effects of simple causal chains and simple temporal orderings, insisting not so much on an atemporal causation as on a causation that is multivariate (A, B, and C together affect D) and multidirectional (A may affect B at one moment, whereas B may affect A at another). The key feature of this systems view is the causal interdependence among multiple systemic forces, all of which act mutually and more or less simultaneously on each other rather than acting unidirectionally and in turn. In any case, a systems view of causality has not yet threatened let alone replaced the classical Humean position as the dominant causal logic in our field. And, more importantly for our purposes here, this view would not greatly alter the key temporal issues embedded within that logic even if it did become the dominant view.

Time Intervals and Causal Explanation

The role of time in our causal explanations does not lie merely in specifying a temporal ordering in which the effect follows the cause in time. The implication of such an ordering is that some **temporal interval**—some *specific amount* of time—is necessary and sufficient for the cause to have the impact that we are going to label the effect. That is, the cause must precede the effect in time because it takes some finite amount of time for the causal process(es) to unfold. That causal process time may be very short, as when reacting to a sudden noise, or very long, as when reacting to an advertising message. But that time is never zero, nor infinity.

Consider, for example, a system involving a set of events at time 1, another set of events at time 2, still another at time 3, and so on. What our Humean methodology tries to do is to isolate one (or each of several) events at time 1 as cause and then measure it's effects on one (or several) of the events at time 2 (or at time 3, time 4, etc.). At the heart of our experimental designs is the imposition of a treatment (at time 1) followed by the measurement of the treatment's effect (at time 2). Some designs also involve other measurements preceding the imposition of the treatment, and some involve other measurements following the initial measurement of the effects (i.e., at times 3, 4, and so on).

If this is to be construed as a cause/effect relation, however, it is in the interval between time 1 and time 2 that the causal process must be realized. That is, there is some finite amount of time, from time 1 to time 2, that is necessary and sufficient for the causal process to unfold. Most processes do not occur instantaneously, although some may occur in a time period too small to be measured with any given technology. Therefore, the interval between time 1 and time 2 must be some finite amount of time.

More often than not, however, the duration of the interval between cause and effect is left unspecified both in our theoretical formulations and in our interpretation of concrete findings. Our methodological procedures generally offer no guidelines for specifying this interval. In the physical sciences, there can sometimes be an observable change in the phenomenon under study (e.g., a color change may indicate that a chemical reaction has occurred—a visible marker of the time needed for the causal process to have its effect). In the behavioral sciences, however, such visible changes are relatively rare. More often, the interval of time between imposition of a treatment and the measurement of its effects is based on arbitrary factors (such as experimenter convenience, or procedures used in previous studies of the same problem) rather than on any theoretical hypotheses about the processes involved.

Our Humean logic of causal reasoning involves yet another temporal assumption: There can be no action at a temporal distance, so to speak. Although there must be some finite amount of time between cause and effect, that interval must be filled—more or less exactly—with the operation of the causal process(es) involved. (In physics this is sometimes referred to as local causation; e.g., Pagels, 1982.) Too great a separation in time weakens the plausibility of the causal link between two events, unless that entire separation is filled with the causal process.

There can be serious interpretive consequences if the duration of this finite time is specified incorrectly. If the interval is set too short, the cause may not yet have had time to yield the intended effects that are to be observed. For instance, a change in diet may not show its effect on cholesterol in the bloodstream after only a single week. If the interval is set too long, the effects of interest may have come and gone, or they may already have been altered by counterforces in the system. For example, an advertising message about a new detergent is unlikely to have an effect on consumer behavior if the measurement of behavior is taken after a year, since the message is likely to have been forgotten by then, and behavior is likely to be influenced by a more recent message. (Further interpretive problems can arise if the effect traces a cyclic or other nonmonotonic form over time. These problems will be dealt with in a later section.)

Temporal Versus Causal Distances

All of these considerations make it clear that we must specify the duration of the intervals that are necessary and sufficient for the unfolding of causal processes, as well as identify the temporal order of postulated causes and effects. This is often difficult to do. Furthermore, that conceptual and practical difficulty is compounded by an intuitive bias in behavioral science and in our culture (already mentioned earlier in this chapter) favoring the idea that the closer together a cause and effect are in time (and space), the more confident we can be about the soundness of our causal interpretation.

This contiguity bias is a part of the Humean causal argument. As mentioned before, Hume's analysis of causality arrived at the conclusion that the only rational basis we could have for inferring causality from empirical events is temporal or spatial contiguity (along with a cause-then-effect temporal order). But that analysis further concluded that, although rational, this basis is also ultimately inadequate to infer any *necessary* connection between the putative cause and its alleged effect. Our willingness to make such causal inferences, stronger ones than we can logically justify, is, according to Hume, merely cultural custom. We *want* to make strong causal inferences. Some would argue we *need* to make them in order to smooth out the business of living—that is, we need a certain amount of predictability. And since we have no better basis for making causal inferences, we tend to accept the only rational—though nonlogical—basis we can find: contiguity in time and space.

There is, of course, some truth in the idea of temporal contiguity as a cue to causality. The closer together cause and effect are in time, the less opportunity there is. for other factors to operate. Hence the less opportunity there is for such intervening events either to obscure or enhance the cause/effect relation being studied, or to present the investigator with a spurious relation that is mistaken for the one being studied. (This is discussed more fully later in this book.) What this ignores, of course, is that some chains of causal processes may take a longer time to unfold than others.

Consider, for example, the following causal sequence of events. A little boy hits a little girl. She drops her skateboard. It rolls off the porch and trips a person on the sidewalk. That person falls into the street in front of an oncoming car. The car swerves to avoid the fallen person, and thereupon hits a second, parked car. What does it mean to draw the causal inference that the parked car was hit because the little boy hit the little girl?

The two events—putative cause and putative effect of that cause—are separated in time, and also in functional steps or links in the logical chain. During the time between cause and effect, several other relevant events occurred: the dropping of the skateboard, the pedestrian tripping, the swerving of the first car. Our causal inference, that the hitting of the parked car was caused by the hitting of the little girl, does not really seem to be sound because cause and effect are separated by so many functional links.

The temporal interval is really not so large—perhaps a matter of seconds or a minute between cause and consequence. But the logical interval is many-stepped. What is critical to our inference is not length of time as such, but the extent to which other factors could have played an instigating role. The size of the time interval is simply the size of the window through which those other factors could have entered the situation. Those factors could be within the chain we have listed (e.g., the falling skateboard, the tripped person, the swerving of the oncoming car). Or, they could be other factors in the situation not yet brought into the picture.

For example, if it turned out that the brakes or steering of the moving car were faulty, or that the little girl threw the skateboard, or that the falling person was drunk, those new facts might cloud our causal conclusion—although they would not alter the temporal contiguity of the relevant factors nor the logical sequence of the chained events already included. Or other factors could lie in still earlier antecedent conditions—for instance, if the boy's action was in response to earlier teasing by the little girl—and this, too, might alter our interpretation of the causal processes involved.

Without belaboring this example any further, we can note that all of these considerations confound the temporal and the logical relations involved in the case. We can have logical complexity with temporal contiguity; or logical simplicity with temporal distance; or the other combinations of the two. And although we tend to assign temporal contiguity a key role in our willingness to make causal inferences, it may well be the logical contiguity that is the more telling feature of such situations. (As a final note on this example: If this were a legal case, the judge would have to rule partly on the basis of foreseeable consequences. That is, the little boy would be assigned causal responsibility only if the little boy [or any reasonable man (sic)] could foresee that his action [hitting the girl] would result in the chain of events leading to the hitting of the parked car. This, also, gives logical directness a more prominent role than literal temporal contiguity.)

But although logical contiguity seems more important than the sheer temporal distance, even in this example both temporal order and temporal contiguity are still crucial in the operation of the causal processes. There is no action at a distance, in either a temporal or a logical interpretation of distance.

It is easy to find counter examples of the temporal contiguity principle. The alleged and much debated sleeper effect (Hovland & Weiss, 1951) in attitude- change research is a case in point. The sleeper effect asserts that, when a persuasive message is delivered by a low-credibility source, the message will not have much impact until enough time has passed so that the source of the message is forgotten, but the message itself is remembered. Here, the interval between the presumed cause (the message) and the predicted effect (the attitude change) is long indeed—often a matter of months. And much of the problem in establishing the **validity** of the sleeper effect stems from the interpretive problems associated with: (a) determining how long this interval needs to be, and (b) dealing with the effects of other factors that might come into play during it.

The validity of any inference about a cause/effect sleeper-effect relation is threatened because many different events could have occurred in the interval to produce the attitude change. The person may have been exposed to other persuasive messages, or may have been prompted to discuss the issue with friends whose views helped produce the attitude change, or may simply have been sensitized to the view expressed in the initial communication, hence more receptive to it when it appeared in other messages. Each of these possible intervening events either weakens or makes more complex the causal linkage between the original message and the ultimate attitude change.

Note, however, that a strong theoretical basis for predicting long-term effects, one that can be disproved or supported by empirical evidence, could help confirm the validity of such effects. Again, it is important to specify theoretically and to confirm empirically the temporal interval necessary for the unfolding of the inferred causal processes.

ASSUMPTIONS FROM THE NATURAL SCIENCES

Much of what is considered proper empirical methodology in the natural sciences may be inappropriate for the study of human behavior. For one thing, temporal features of the processes underlying human behavior often take place in a different time domain that is far more macro than the critical events in many areas of physical science. Furthermore, many of the dominant conceptualizations in social and behavioral science hold that human motivation involves factors (e.g., goals, expectations, intentions) that presumably do not apply to physical forces or even to members of many other biological species. Yet most of our research design and methodology is borrowed directly from these other sciences, and the assumptions underlying those paradigms are usually incorporated into our work without being questioned. Two pairs of assumptions about natural processes are particularly important in regard to specifying temporal intervals between causal treatments and measurements of effects: (a) that processes are inertial and linear, and (b) that change is instantaneous and persistent.

Assumptions of Inertial and Linear Processes

We have a strong bias in our methodology to assume that change processes occur in a manner that is monotonic, linear, and stable across time. We tend to assume that there is an inertial feature (a continuance of the motion) regarding the direction of change, and that there is always some kind of proportionality between the length of the time interval between cause and effect and the amount of change in the effect. That is, if we find a certain amount of change from time 1 to time 2, which we take to be a function of a particular cause, then we would tend to assume that we would find proportionally more change in the same direction for the interval from time 1 to time 3, assuming time 3 is temporally more distant than time 2. This is sometimes assumed even when the cause is a one-time manipulation, and almost always assumed when the manipulation involves the onset of some continuing process. (The temporal form of causal treatments are discussed in the next section of this chapter and in Chapter 4.)

Even if linear, monotonic functions are prevalent in the natural sciences, there is mounting evidence that such smooth functions are not adequate to describe many behavioral processes. Much of human behavior is cyclic in nature. In fact, some biologists now claim that **rhythmic** coordination between biological processes is the fundamental organizing principle of life. If behavioral processes also occur as cycles or **oscillations**, rather than as linear functions, then most of our research methodology is inadequate to measure these processes.

Imagine a behavioral process that traces a smooth **sine wave** and that is set in motion (or caused) by a particular treatment imposed by the researcher. In a traditional research design, only one measurement of the effect is taken after the treatment is imposed. In this case, totally opposite conclusions about the effects of the treatment can be arrived at depending on whether the interval between the treatment and the measurement of the effect places that measurement point at a peak or at an ebb in the curve. If the measurement is taken at the peak of the curve, then the conclusion would be that the treatment had a positive effect. If the measurement is taken at the ebb of the curve, then the conclusion would be that the treatment had a negative effect. A null conclusion would be drawn if the measurement was taken between the peak and the ebb of the curve. This discussion will be elaborated in the next section. At this point, it will suffice to say that our logic of method is based in part on an assumption of linear change processes, an assumption that may not be adequate to describe much of human behavior.

Assumptions of Instantaneous and Persistent Change

A second pair of assumptions handed down from the natural sciences is that change occurs more or less instantaneously, and that it is persistent (that is, that ordinarily the change will persist unless deliberate steps are taken to reverse the change process). Such changes are plentiful in the natural sciences, and they tend to make time of observation a less critical factor. For instance, many of the reactions caused by mixing chemicals occur faster than the human eye can detect, and many result in new forms that are relatively stable. In this case, whether you observe the end result of the process five seconds after or five minutes after the change has occurred, the conclusion arrived at would be the same.

In human behavior, however, it is not always the case that changes are instantaneous; nor that a change, once established, will persist. A change in attitude may take place over a period of time rather than all at once. Decisions are not all made instantly. Yet our theories seldom specify the amount of time needed for such changes to occur; hence, by default, they imply that the change does occur all at once. If we assume that change is instantaneous, then there is no need for theoretical statements about the time course of causal processes. Furthermore, a single measurement of the effect, at some point in time after the treatment has been imposed, is sufficient for describing the (instantaneous and persistent) effect of that treatment on the variables of interest.

In contrast, if we assume that behavioral change is a process that takes time, then a single measurement of the behavior is inadequate to describe that process. And the interpretations arrived at on the basis of that single measurement will be a function of the point in time chosen (usually arbitrarily) to measure the effect. (This point will be elaborated later in this chapter.)

As to the persistence of changes: Not all behavior processes are continuously in an on state, with or without the intervention of **experimental treatments**. Many processes at physiological, psychological, and social behavior levels reflect intermittent, oscillating, cyclical states. For example: When people talk to each other, no one of them talks incessantly. Rather, the participants in a conversation take turns, oscillating between speaking and silence—and there is ample evidence that the temporal patterning of that oscillation reflects many features of that dyad and the context in which they are behaving (see Dabbs, 1983; Warner, 1984; McGrath & Kelly, 1986). But the possibility of nonpersistent changes (that is, oscillating or cyclical processes) is also assumed away by studies for which we have only one posttreatment measure, and in theories that omit reference to the time-course of the hypothesized cause/effect relation.

THE TEMPORAL SHAPE OF CAUSAL PROCESSES

The duration of the X-Y interval is worth closer examination. If we assume that a causal process takes place in the time between X and Y, then we must be concerned with the **temporal shape** of that process. That is, we need to consider how the length of time from X to Y affects the resulting pattern of changes in Y, hence the conclusions that we draw about the meaning of the X-Y events of our study.

Figure 1.1 illustrates some of the different shapes that behavioral processes may trace over time. Some of them are not in accord with the assumptions about change that we have borrowed from the physical sciences (as discussed earlier in this chapter).

(a) a gradually increasing, linear process,
(b) an all-at-once change that is then maintained over time (persistent, in the earlier discussion),
(c) an all-at-once change that is not maintained over time (not persistent),
(d) a delayed effect (not instantaneous), and
(e) a cyclical process (neither inertial nor linear).

Assume that an initial observation, O_1, is made on a particular dependent variable prior to the imposition of a treatment, X. (In Figure 1.1, all processes are shown with a pretreatment result at the same baseline value.) Assume further that the investigator has the option of making measurements on the dependent variable after the treatment at any of the following times, O_2, O_3, and O_4. Figure 1.1 illustrates that the conclusion that the investigator draws on the basis of a single subsequent measurement will depend on both: (1) which interval is chosen for comparison (O_1 to O_2, O_1 to O_3, or O_1 to O_4); and (2) the shape of the process being examined.

If the causal process is linear and gradually increasing, as in process a, then the conclusion about the magnitude of the cause/effect relation will depend on whether the final measurement is taken at O_2, O_3, or O_4. For example, there will be a conclusion of a greater effect of X if the second measurement is taken at O_4 rather than at O_2.

If the causal process unfolds immediately and exerts its effects immediately on the processes being measured, as in process b. in the figure, then the conclusion about the cause/effect relation will be the same regardless of when the final measurement is taken.

More serious complication arise for process c. Here, the investigator would conclude that X had a large effect if the measurement were taken at O_2, a moderate effect if the measurement were taken at O_3, and no effect if the measurement were taken at O_4.

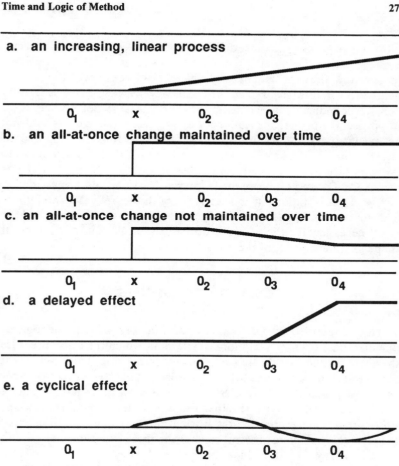

Figure 1.1   Temporal Shapes of the Outcome Process, Y

Conversely, for process d, measurements at O_2 and O_3 would lead the investigator to conclude that no effect had occurred, whereas measurement at O_4 would identify the effect. (Note, however, that even if a post measure was taken at O_4, the investigator would still not know that the effect was delayed unless at least two measurements were made after the treatment—either O_2 and O_4, or O_3 and O_4. Nor would the investigator know in the case of process c that the effect deteriorated with time, unless some additional measures were taken.)

Process e poses a still more difficult problem. With this cyclic process, a single measurement at O_2, when the cycle is at its peak, would indicate that the treatment exerted a large, positive effect on the process being measured. Measurement at O_4, however, when the cycle is at its ebb, would indicate that the treatment exerted a large, negative effect on the process. Further, measurement at O_3, when the cycle is midway between its peak and its ebb, would indicate that the treatment had no effect. (Note that the investigator would probably not be aware of the cyclic nature of the process being observed unless all three measurements, O_2, O_3, and O_4, were made, plus at least one additional one.)

Clearly, it is important to specify, in both theoretical formulations and empirical practices, both the time interval between the cause and the effect necessary for the causal processes to unfold, and the temporal shape, or time-course, of the process under observation.

CONCLUDING COMMENTS

This chapter has argued that temporal factors pervade the logic of our methods. A known temporal relation, in which the cause precedes the effect in time, is at the base of our causal reasoning. This implies that some finite amount of time between a cause and its effect is necessary for the causal processes to unfold. Strong causal conclusions require a more precise specification of the length of this temporal interval and the shape of the process under observation. Furthermore, a single measurement of the effect is usually insufficient to describe these causal processes.

Thus far, we have introduced only a few of many temporal issues that are intricately woven into the fabric of the methodology of our field. In the next two chapters we will open many more such temporal issues, first at the macro level of **research strategy** and **study design**, then at the more micro level of manipulation and measurement of variables. Then, in the last two chapters of the book, we will try to describe some of the ways such temporal issues can be taken into account in social and behavioral science research.

2

Temporal Issues in Strategy, Design, and Validity of Studies

Temporal issues are involved in all aspects of our methodology. At a relatively macro level, there are a number of temporal factors that play an important role in choices of research strategy and in implementation of those choices. Temporal issues arise, as well, in the design of studies and in their organization so as to yield valid findings. It is the temporal factors in these macrolevel features of research strategy and design, and of the search for valid findings, that we will examine in this chapter, leaving to a later chapter those temporal features arising at more microlevels of study procedure.

The first part of the chapter focuses on temporal issues in the choice of research strategies, that is, in the choice of settings in which the research will take place. Research settings differ in many regards. One important way they differ is in terms of the **temporal context** of the setting. Some studies take place in a natural temporal context, in which processes are allowed to unfold at a natural rate; some take place in a temporal context that is experimentally contrived by the researcher. The choice of how to treat the temporal context of a study, which reflects the researcher's temporal biases and assumptions, has far reaching effects on the information that can be derived from that study.

The second part of the chapter focuses on temporal issues in study design. Study design refers to the researcher's plan for arranging treatments and observations in a study. Temporal features are crucial to the logic of design. Each interval between an observation and a treatment can be considered a **temporal window** through which can operate both intended causal processes and unintended events that may enhance, obscure, or attenuate the causal processes. Proper research design, therefore, requires an effective match between: (a) the treatment to observation intervals, and (b) the durations of the causal processes to be studied. That match must allow the causal processes to unfold fully, without having yet begun to fade, and without unnecessary contamination by extraneous events.

Many of the extraneous events that can enter through the various temporal windows involved in a research design can be regarded as **plausible rival hypotheses**; as explanations of study results, they are rivals to hypotheses involving the causal treatments that the investigator is exploring in the study. These extraneous factors that give rise to plausible rival hypotheses can be regarded as "threats to the validity" of the study (Campbell & Stanley, 1966). Most of those threats to the validity of a study are profoundly temporal in nature, and are affected by the size of the temporal window. The third part of this chapter presents a discussion of temporal features of some of those threats to the **internal validity** of a study, and the chapter closes with a brief discussion of temporal issues in **external validity,** emphasizing the generalizability of findings over time.

THE TEMPORAL CONTEXT OF RESEARCH STRATEGIES

Observations of behavior can be made in a variety of settings, some that are naturally occurring and some that are artificial. **Research strategies** refer to these general settings within which research can be conducted. Runkel and McGrath (1972) have identified eight classes of research strategies: **field studies, field experiments, experimental simulations, laboratory experiments, judgment studies, sample surveys, formal theories** and **computer simulations.** We will follow their terminology and distinctions in this book.

Eight Research Strategies

These strategies vary on a number of different dimensions. For instance, they vary in how much they permit **control** by the researcher over possible confounding variables, in how much they allow precision of measurement of the variables of interest, in how much they provide

realism of the context within which the research is taking place, and in how much they permit **generalization** of study results to different populations.

These dimensions reflect methodological trade-offs. Realism, the degree to which the context of the study is natural to the participants, is especially important here. Strategies differ markedly in this respect. But the very strategies that are high in realism tend to be low in precision and control. And precision of measurement and control of variables is a sine qua non for strong quantitative results.

Field studies, for example, take place in natural settings and therefore generally allow for high realism of the context within which the study participants are behaving. But field studies generally offer little control over other extraneous variables, less precision in the measurement of the variables of interest, and little generalization to populations outside that natural setting. Field experiments generally have the same advantages and disadvantages as field studies. Field experiments differ from field studies, however, in that the investigator intrudes on the natural environment to the extent of making a deliberate manipulation of one or more variables. The setting loses naturalness to the degree that those manipulations are intrusive.

Experimental simulations and laboratory studies differ sharply from field studies and field experiments on the dimensions of realism, precision of measurement and generalizability. They are done in experimentally created settings. However, experimental simulations involve a deliberate attempt on the part of the experimenter to recreate or mirror a naturally occurring behavioral system. They can be relatively high in realism of context to the extent that the simulation accurately reflects the system that it is intended to mirror. But they are still low in realism of context in the sense that the participants are not naturally occurring parts of the system (i.e., they are brought into the setting by the experimenter). Laboratory experiments, on the other hand, occur in settings that are intended to highlight certain behavioral processes while minimizing the effects of other processes by a deliberate stripping away of the natural context for the behavioral processes. Thus, they are generally very low in realism of context. However, both experimental simulations and laboratory experiments offer greater control over possibly confounding variables and greater precision of measurement of the behaviors of interest.

Sample surveys and judgment tasks are not research settings per se, but are strategies for collecting behavioral observations in situations in which the behavior in question is not intrinsically connected to the setting. In these strategies, the setting is regarded as extraneous to the behavioral observations rather than as being a determinant of that behavior. The final two strategies in the Runkel and McGrath schema, computer simulations and formal theory, are not empirical strategies, and therefore they do not refer to any particular substantive context.

These strategies involve other strengths and weaknesses. All of the strategies involve decisions that must be faced about the richness of the information desired, the cost of the study in terms of labor, money, and equipment, and so forth. And all of the strategies involve trade-offs among realism, precision, and generalizability. A researcher must be aware of the strengths and weaknesses of the particular strategy that he or she is using, and should attempt to complement one strategy with others across a series of studies. (For further discussion of these, see Runkel & McGrath, 1972; Cook & Campbell, 1979.) This chapter will explore an additional dimension, quite important to the realism of the experimental situation, upon which these strategies can differ: the treatment of time in the study context.

Temporal Features of Research Strategies

The research strategies differ, especially, in terms of the naturalness, or realism, of the setting within which observations are made. Field studies and field experiments take place in natural settings that exist prior to and after the observations of the study have taken place, and that exist independent of the researcher's purposes. Furthermore, participants are in the setting for reasons of their own, not for purposes of the investigator. Laboratory studies and experimental simulations, on the other hand, occur in settings that are artificial from the point of view of the participants, and that have been created for the purposes of the research.

These strategies differ in a parallel fashion in terms of how they treat the temporal part of that setting. That is, the strategies differ in the degree to which they allow the behavioral processes under observation to occur in **real time** or force them to take place in **experimental time**. Real time or **system time** conditions refer to the time it would take for the behaviors to unfold naturally, in their normal setting. Experimental time conditions refers to the temporal context artificially created for the study.

Experimental time can involve modification of either of two sets of temporal parameters: Temporal order of events, and duration of events and the intervals between them. First, it can involve a change in the temporal ordering or sequencing of events from what would have occurred naturally in the behavioral system. In fact, part of the point of conducting an experiment is to control the time order of the putative cause and its expected effect. When the experimenter introduces a manipulation into the environment, that in effect fixes a temporal sequence of cause—then—effect so that causal conclusions may be appropriate.

A change in the ordering of events is a fundamental feature of experimental design that is used to allow the investigator to draw strong inferences about causal relations among the events under study. The cause must precede the effect in time in order for a causal inference to be drawn, and fixing the order of these two events makes such an inference possible. This type of temporal change can be used with any of the research strategies that permit experimental manipulations—field experiments, experimental simulations, laboratory experiments, sample surveys, and judgment studies.

The second meaning of experimental time involves a change in the duration of events and of the intervals between events from what would have occurred naturally. For example, when the experimenter presents a series of slides at a rate of one-per-minute to a group of participants, the experimenter is changing those durations and intervals from what might be a more natural (and irregular) pace for those participants. Such changes in the duration of events and intervals between events occurs primarily in settings over which the investigator has a high degree of control, such as in laboratory experiments and experimental simulations. Here, most frequently, the experimenter telescopes (collapses) real time, by introducing time limits and deadlines for the events being studied. By careful sequencing and timing of events, the investigator packs more events into an experimental session than might occur in the same amount of time under natural conditions. For instance, an experimenter who is interested in studying jury decision making might control the presentation of evidence and arguments in the case, and limit the time given for reaching a decision, so that the entire session can take place within a manageable experimental period. Thus, the experimenter telescopes the operation of system processes into an "experimental hour."

In general, use of real time versus experimental time varies with the degree of naturalness of the experimental context. In the natural context of field studies and field experiments, for example, the behavior under study goes forward in real time—that is, the time it takes system events to unfold under normal or natural conditions. But unlike field studies, field experiments generally fix the temporal ordering of at least one set of events in order to be able to draw causal conclusions. In the concocted settings of laboratory experiments and experimental simulations, on the other hand, the behaviors under study unfold within an experimental time that is part of the experimental concoction that establishes the setting.

Two other settings—judgment studies and sample surveys—involve conditions that attempt to blunt or eliminate the effects of context, to make the behavior being observed as nearly context-free as possible. In these strategies, sequences of events do not unfold in time at all. Rather, more or less timeless questions get answered in sequences and with time lags that are merely artifacts of the procedures themselves. To be sure, the behaviors involved in those responses—perhaps verbal answers, perhaps behavior choices—take some finite amount of time. But the duration and timing of those responses are artificially isolated from other system events, and are regarded largely as a function of only the immediately preceding stimulus pattern.

Finally, the two nonempirical strategies—formal theories and computer simulations—literally have no behavior in them and hence have no temporal behavioral context either. Time enters into formal theory only in a conceptual sense, and then only if the theory contains important temporal features (e.g., sequencing of events). Computer simulations may contain important elements of temporal processes within the formulation of the model. That is, the simulation may mirror complex system dynamics. But the temporal course of the operation of a run of the simulation does not represent the unfolding of system events, but the unfolding of the model of system events.

As with overall choice of research strategies, there are advantages and disadvantages to using real time versus experimental time in any particular research study. Studying processes in real time can lead to more information about the temporal shape of the processes and their effects in a real-life context—provided we can unconfound the processes from one another and from extraneous factors. That is a huge proviso. Furthermore, real time observations are costly in time and resources.

Studying a process in experimental time, on the other hand, may be more efficient in terms of personnel time and other resources. However, doing so always risks distortion of the process being studied—for example, by altering the temporal course and shape of a causal process through the imposition of deadlines. There is no way to know whether the process under study is the same or different from what would have unfolded under natural temporal circumstances (e.g., would a jury decision that is made under a one-hour deadline be the same one that would be reached when no deadline is imposed?).

Real Time Versus Experimental
Time in Research Strategies

Some of the consequences of these differences in temporal context are worth closer examination. In field studies, the direct observations that often constitute the major data collection of that strategy must take place on line (where and when they occur) hence in real time. The events being observed are taking place in, and being recorded during, what can reasonably be described as natural temporal patterns. No artificial time constraints are used; the ordering and sequencing of events is left undisturbed. What takes place and when it takes place is determined, not by the concoctions of the experimenter but by the ongoing processes of the real-world system that is being studied. What is observed, however, is determined by the investigator, and it has at least two temporal facets: (a) the duration of the period of system action that is to be studied is temporally bounded by the length of the observation period; and (b) the temporal differentiation between events that can be dealt with is bounded by the temporal precision with which observations are made.

Field experiments, though still taking place in natural settings, add some artificiality to the situation, and some of that artificiality involves temporal features. The settings and behaviors in general are natural with respect to temporal context. By design, however, the experimenter has disturbed the natural ordering of at least one important set of events, by introducing a manipulation of an independent variable into the system. The behaviors being observed are allowed to unfold in real time, and to follow their natural temporal pattern, except that the experimenter (by virtue of the experimental intervention) has introduced a predetermined order relation with respect to one particular set of system events (the manipulated X and the reputed effect, Y) so that a directional causal inference can be made about them.

Incidentally, such an experimental intervention has two additional, though subtle, side effects. First, it tends to make any possible ahistoric-systemic interpretation moot, since causal directionality, at least in regard to X, is fixed by the experimenter and multiple and bidirectional relations involving X are precluded (whether or not the natural system might have shown them). Second, experimental manipulation of X also makes the causal-chain interpretation of relations involving X in part a self-fulfilling prophecy, since directional relations from X to Y can occur but other relations involving X cannot. Thus, results of experiments involving manipulation of some system variables do not really distinguish between historical and ahistorical causal systems; they merely assume that the former holds and the latter does not.

Experimental simulations take the control of temporal orderings one step further. In this strategy, the investigator creates an artificial setting that attempts to mirror the class of natural systems that is being modeled. The experimenter has full control over the introduction of events into the system, including the duration of events and of intervals between events, and temporal ordering of events in relation to one another. The investigator has the option of mirroring real time, creating an experimental time, or combining these two time scales in some fashion, as the temporal context for the unfolding of events during the simulation.

In a flight simulator, for example, the experimenter may introduce wind gusts, system failures, an unexpected obstacle, and the like, in any temporal order that suits experimental purposes, in order to test the pilot's and the system's reactions to those events. In this strategy the experimenter often makes some use of an experimental time, for instance by telescoping the amount of real flight time it would take to encounter all the events introduced. But the investigator tries to keep real time relations between microlevel processes (such as the timing between wind buffets and the wind speeds involved in them) as they are in the natural system, because time to correct specific perturbations is a crucial performance variable in a flight simulation. The experimenter's hope is that telescoping the time between macrolevel events does not affect the pilot's responses to those microlevel perturbations.

In other experimental simulations, such as "in basket" tests of managerial skill or mock jury decision-making tasks, the experimenter deliberately telescopes the operating time of the simulation—for instance by requiring that a verdict be reached within a single hour of deliberation, or that all the problems in the basket be resolved today. In this case, experimental time of the simulation is much more like the operating time in laboratory experiments.

Many studies of basic psychological processes—such as perception, cognition, problem-solving speed, and the like—are called laboratory studies because they take place in rooms called laboratories and make use of experimental designs. But most of them are judgment studies in the Runkel and McGrath (1972) terminology being used here. In such studies, basic processes are studied in ways that preserve real-time relations in the actual behaviors themselves (such as the perceiving of a presented stimulus, the arithmetic calculations needed to solve a problem), just as real time is preserved among the microlevel events in experimental simulations. But very strong experimental constraints are imposed on such matters as stimulus order and exposure time, and other surrounding macrolevel features of the situation. Indeed, in such judgment studies, the context, including the temporal context, is made moot insofar as possible. (This point is discussed further later in this section.)

But most studies that are actually laboratory experiments in the Runkel and McGrath terminology operate in a totally artificial experimental time. In most cases, the times of natural processes are telescoped to fit events into shorter, more convenient experimental periods. In most cases, too, the time constraints placed on the sequences of experimental events are chosen, not to reflect temporal patterns found in natural settings, and not to reflect temporal patterns derived from theory, but to fit into the experimental hour, or to be consistent with the times used for the same experimental tasks in previous studies. Laboratory experiments attempt to study generic processes apart from a natural context. Whether or not the temporal context should be considered either as an intrinsic part of the process or as noise is seldom closely examined. Rather, the temporal context is established, along with other aspects of the setting, largely for experimental convenience.

Some laboratory experiments (and, potentially, experimental simulations and judgment studies as well) make an opposite transformation between real time and experimental time: They expand rather than telescope the time involved in some of the processes being studied. An example would be the use of process-tracing techniques that generate protocols by asking respondents to "think out loud," hence to make some aspects of their internal cognitive processes available to the experimenter. In these, the processes under study actually take much longer to complete than they would under natural conditions; and again, there has been little inquiry into how such time transformations alter the processes that are being assessed.

Laboratory researchers in social psychology, for the most part, have not been interested enough in time to manipulate it as an important independent variable. But they have recognized that permitting time (especially task performance times) to vary naturally could introduce substantial noise into the experimental data. So they generally have controlled time by holding time intervals constant, counterbalancing orders of presentation, and so forth. By these experimental operations—controlling and counterbalancing—they ensure that no differences resulting from time will affect their results. At the same time, the high level of control over both time order and time of occurrence of events, that is potentially available in laboratory settings, would make it possible to test very precise specifications of temporal intervals involved in hypothesized causal processes. It is therefore doubly to be regretted that so few of those laboratory experiments give attention to the study of such temporal factors.

In both judgment studies and sample surveys, the responses being observed are elicited by the experimenter's questions or stimuli and are not responses to the ongoing dynamics of the behavior setting. In both of these strategies, some temporal factors, such as order of stimuli, are carefully controlled. In sample surveys, order of questions is often held constant for convenience in reproducing the survey materials, as well as because of a generalized bias in favor of **standardization.** In judgment studies, sequence and timing of stimuli are sometimes controlled because they are of interest and sometimes counterbalanced because leaving them free to vary might introduce error into results.

Although collection of data takes some finite amount of time in both of these strategies, whether or not the responses are produced in real time is not really an applicable question. The responses themselves are artificial; that is, they are creatures of the research situation and generally would not occur at all outside of the study situation. Hence, we cannot really determine whether or not they occurred in the time natural to them in real situations. Time is important in these strategies, but only as a property of the research study itself, in terms of exercising control over features of the research situation. In sample surveys, it is crucial to prevent the infusion of irrelevant or unmeasured outside factors by not spreading data collection over too long a period of time. In judgment studies, it is important to control the order of stimuli and to measure response times.

For formal theories, talking about real time versus experimental time does not make sense. There are no **actors-behaving-in-context** (Runkel & McGrath, 1972) in these strategies. Time enters into theories only conceptually, if and when time is an important substantive variable in the theory (an occasion far too infrequent in our view). Formal theory in the behavioral sciences has relied much more on verbal than on mathematical formulations, perhaps discouraging the specification of quantified temporal intervals.

Time, however, plays an unusual role in computer simulations. Again, there are no actors-behaving-in-context. But, like the experimental simulation, computer simulations involve an attempt to mirror the dynamics of the system being simulated. Those system dynamics are likely to have important temporal features, including both order and interval relations among variables. The simulation operates in its own time frame (in computer time, so to speak), usually much faster than real time or even most uses of experimental time.

Fidelity of the simulation, one aspect of validity for that strategy, requires that those temporal order and interval relations within the system dynamics be preserved in the output of the simulation—though not necessarily in a form directly observable in the ongoing simulation process. Protocol matching to assess the validity of the simulation does not require that the temporal orderings and intervals within the simulation have any necessary relation to the orderings of the system processes they are attempting to mirror; it simply requires that the output of the simulation (the protocol) match the output of the natural process.

Thus, the eight strategies differ among themselves considerably in the way they treat time. Some operate in real time, some in an experimental time. Some attempt to make time irrelevant to the data. Some reflect time only in symbolic form. And all of these time differences play into the logic of causal inference that was discussed in the first chapter. If causal inference requires specification of an order of events, and if causal explanation requires specification of a time interval for the operation of causal processes, then it does make a difference how time is treated in our research settings. Experimental time is not the same as real time. If an experiment is intended to be a representation of a generic class of real world systems, concocted in order to study analogues of real world processes, then it is essential that the experimental time used in that analogue bear some specifiable relation to time as it operates within those real world processes. It is essential, in other words, to be able to *transpose* temporal order and interval relations between real time or system time and experimental time.

Almost no real world system processes operate in neat, one-link-of-the-chain-at-a-time fashion. Almost none of them operate so that the stimulus on one trial is independent of the response on the preceding trial—a characteristic that differentiates laboratory experiments, judgment studies and sample surveys, on the one hand, from field experiments, field studies and experimental simulations on the other. Almost no real world processes operate so that intervals between events: (a) are arbitrary (that is, do not depend on system forces); or (b) are of no consequence. And almost none of them operate so as to fit conveniently into an experimental hour. Yet, the social and behavioral science literature seems to reflect very little methodological effort devoted to trying to figure out how best to transpose between real time and experimental time, while preserving some of the essential temporal features of the system processes that are being studied.

TEMPORAL FACTORS IN STUDY DESIGN

Research design refers to the sets of choices researchers make in planning the treatments and observations that will be included in a study. One central concern in developing such a research plan is to make sure the design will permit the drawing of valid conclusions about causal relations. No design is perfect. Yet some are open to more and more serious threats to the validity of causal inferences than others.

In general, threats to the validity of a study represent plausible alternative hypotheses that rival the hypotheses under study as potential explanations for the relations found in the study. In other words, they represent alternative ways to account for the evidence that the study generates without invoking the cause/effect relation contained in the investigator's hypotheses or interpretations.

Many of these threats to validity of a study are temporal in nature; and many of the causes and corrections for these threats are also temporal in nature. These will be the topic of later parts of this chapter, under the headings of **internal validity** and **external validity.** Before moving to that discussion, it is worth considering some general features of study designs and of the temporal patterns they involve.

How Time Affects Study Designs

The most primitive study design is the pattern that Campbell and Stanley (1966) refer to as the one-shot design and regard euphemistically as a preexperimental design rather than a true experiment. (A **true experiment** [a] must contain at least two conditions, with one or more of those conditions involving an experimental treatment and [b] must use a random procedure for allocating cases to conditions.) (See glossary for **randomization**.) This one-shot design calls for a single group of cases to be observed after they have all received a specific treatment. Even here, the temporal order required for causal interpretation is preserved. Since knowledge is knowledge of differences, however, we cannot interpret such an effect without some other basis for comparison.

One way to get such a comparison basis would be to collect a set of pretest observations before the experimental treatment. The pretest observations must precede both the treatment and the posttest observations in time. The difference between the pretest and the posttest observations provides some comparative leverage for interpreting the effect of the treatment.

This second design is also one that Campbell and Stanley label preexperimental, and it too is fraught with flaws. A number of those flaws are reflected in threats to validity that have a temporal form. For example, since this design gets its comparative leverage by comparing two sets of observations that bracket the experimental treatment in time, that same temporal interval makes room for the entry of any of a number of extraneous factors that can obscure the relation being studied. (See later parts of this chapter.)

Let us now assume that a relatively powerful design is used. Let us further assume that the design is a true experiment, one that employs not only a pre- and postcomparison, but also comparisons between the experimental group and one or more **control groups** that did not receive any experimental treatment, and that uses a random procedure (randomization: R) to allocate cases to the different comparison groups. Specifically, let us assume a design in which participants are randomly allocated into two groups: an experimental group (EX) and a control or comparison group (CO). The EX group is to be observed (O_1), then given an experimental treatment (X), and then observed again (O_2). The CO group is to be observed (O_3) at the same time as the EX group's pretreatment observation, O_1, but *not* be given an experimental treatment (X') at the time the EX group is given one, and then observed a second time (O_4) at the same time as the second observation of the experimental group, O_2.

$$\text{Experimental} \ldots \quad | \quad O_1 \; X \; O_2$$
$$R < \quad |$$
$$\text{Comparison} \ldots . \quad | \quad O_3 \; X' \; O_4$$

Adding a comparison group that does not receive the experimental treatment strengthens the investigator's ability to draw valid causal inferences from the design because it allows for a baseline comparison against which some of the temporally based threats can be evaluated. In such a "pretest, posttest, control group" design, however, there is an added set of temporal relations involved in the comparisons. For both groups, the pretest precedes the posttest in time. For the experimental group, the treatment follows the pretest but precedes the posttest. So the pre- to posttime interval defined for the control group is divided into two intervals for the experimental group: a pretest to treatment interval, and a treatment to posttest interval. We noted earlier that researchers need to specify the time intervals involved in their causal interpretations. It is clear that those problems are made more complex as we draw upon more complex study designs.

In the idealized design, the pretest observations for both groups ought to be made simultaneously, and the posttest observations also should be made at the same time for both groups. To the extent that such simultaneity is not achieved, there is an additional temporal interval— the time between when any one wave of observations was made for the various experimental and comparison groups. Factors extraneous to the causal interpretation being explored may come into play for one set of observations, but not for the other. The causal interpretation that is intended in the plan is thereby confounded.

In practice, of course, observations of all of a relatively large number of cases cannot be done simultaneously. Good experimental practice requires that a kind of cross-sectional simultaneity be preserved by ensuring that equal numbers of (randomly chosen) experimental and control cases are premeasured or postmeasured at any one observation session, even though complete data collection may extend over many sessions and many days or months!

Of course, if data collection extends over very long periods of time, even if such cross-sectional simultaneity is preserved by counterbalancing across conditions within observation periods, still other temporal problems may arise. Both outside events (what we will call history later in this chapter) and inside events (what we will later call maturation) may affect results. And although the comparison of experimental and no treatment control groups will help discern the effects of history and maturation, that comparison won't be of much help if history or maturation (or other time-based effects) interacts with the experimental treatment to produce differential effects on postmeasures. (In this context, **interaction** means that the observed effect when both factors are present—e.g., history and the experimental treatment—produces something different from what one would expect if the two separate effects were simply added together.) Furthermore, if the data collection goes on too long, participants in later sessions will almost certainly be aware of what was going on in the early sessions for both experimental and control conditions.

Note that, although this discussion is phrased in terms implying a laboratory experiment, all of these temporal problems, including leakage of knowledge of treatments across conditions, can occur in either laboratory or field settings.

Study Designs as Temporal and Logical Templates

The preceding discussion makes it clear that every study design is an arrangement of temporal orders and intervals of planned research events—observations, and experimental treatments and nontreatments. That arrangement of orders and intervals provides a *template* for interpreting that study's outcomes. In such interpretations, all of the many order relations and intervals within the research arrangements must be taken into account. Those temporal orders and intervals play a role in assessing the plausibility of the cause/effect relations that the investigator wishes to infer. They also play a role in assessing the plausibility of various alternatives (rival hypotheses) that are threats to the investigator's preferred interpretation (including the rival hypothesis that there were no nonchance effects). Those temporal orders and intervals also must be taken into account as part of the investigator's construal of the pattern of processes that best accounts for whatever effects did or did not occur in the study.

Every X-then-Y order relation within a study (that is, every experimental treatment—then—observation sequence) represents both a logical-causal, and a chronological, order relation. Both of those aspects of the order relation must be taken into account in any assessment of the plausibility of the causal relations of interest as well as the plausibility of alternatives. (See glossary for **logical-causal** order.)

At the same time, every temporal order relation in a study that is an X-Y interval represents three important functions that must be reckoned within our interpretations.

(1) The X-Y interval is a causal process interval. The duration of that interval must be taken into account in interpreting the temporal operation of the processes involved in any causal relations. (Causal processes (exactly) fill the cause/effect interval.)

(2) The X-Y interval is a period of time for operation of the system that embeds the experiment. The duration of that period marks the time during which other features of the substantive system are operating and thus can obscure the intended experimental effects. Such obscuring can occur because other system processes produced the experimental effect without benefit of the investigator's intervention, or because such system processes operated to oppose, reverse, enhance, or render moot what otherwise would have been the effects of that intervention in the system.

(3) The X-Y interval is a temporal window for entry of extraneous factors. The magnitude of that window, the time between manipulations and observations, marks the length of time during which various threats to validity of the study's findings could enter and could operate to obscure the intended experimental effects.

To repeat: Every order relation, X-Y, in a study design represents five key functions: It is both a causal and a chronological order relation, and it is a causal process interval, a system process period, and a temporal window for extraneous factors.

Temporal Orders and Intervals in Study Designs

Consider, now, the temporal orders and intervals that are involved in some standard designs that were discussed earlier in this chapter, which are the Campbell and Stanley (1966) design types #1, #2, and #4.

In design #1 (the preexperimental, one-shot design), there is only one temporal order relation (treatment must precede observations), and the one temporal interval associated with that order relation. In design #2 (the pretest/posttest preexperimental design), there are several order relations (hence several intervals): the first set of observations (O_1) precedes both the experimental treatment (X) and the second set of observations (O_2); and the experimental treatment (X) precedes the second set of observations (O_2).

In design #4 (the pretest—posttest—control group true experiment), the number of temporal order relations and time intervals is considerably larger. There is an order relation (and interval) between the first and second observations for each group. There is an order relation (and interval) between the first observation and the experimental treatment, and between the treatment and the second observation, for the experimental group. The two order relations and intervals for this group are: O_1 to X and X to O_2. There are also two similar order relations and intervals for the comparison group—who did not receive the experimental treatment, but nevertheless did have something else occur for them at the same point in time when the experimental group received its treatment. We can refer to that as the experimental nontreatment, symbolize it as X', and recognize that this nontreatment is always there in principle, even though in some studies it would be hard to pin down as a specific set of events. The two order relations and intervals associated with them are O_3 to X' and X' to O_4.

There are two other sets of temporal relations within this design that need to be taken into account. Certain sets of observations are intended to be parallel in time, as well as comparable in other respects, for experimental and comparison conditions. Such simultaneity should hold, for example, for the observations designated as O_1 and O_3 and for those designated as O_2 and O_4 in design #4. (Such simultaneity also should hold for experimentally similar pairings in various other designs). Of course, such simultaneity is indeed both approximate and arbitrary. (See glossary re **simultaneity, succession,** and **synchronization.**) Just how close is close enough is a complex question depending on the sizes, and the meanings, of the time intervals involved. If critical processes are operating at microsecond intervals, then it is in such time units that the approximation of simultaneity must be reckoned. But if the critical processes involved are matters of days or weeks, then the temporal limits on simultaneity of measures are to be reckoned in those grosser temporal units. To the extent that parallel batches do not suffer the research events simultaneously, another temporal window is created through which various extraneous factors can enter and confound study results.

It is implicit in such design formats that any given study event (observation or treatment) is intended to occur approximately simultaneously for all members of any given batch—for example, for the first observation of all members of the experimental group, for the application of the experimental treatment to all members of that group, for the first observation of all members of the control condition, and so on. Of course, as we have already noted, with any relatively large number of cases per batch, even approximate simultaneity is impossible. Researchers usually try to handle this problem by temporal counterbalancing—running an approximately equal number of (randomly chosen) cases of each condition during each time interval, thereby making subsets of cases temporally parallel across comparison batches. This has the unintended side effect, of course, of introducing some additional temporal order relations and temporal intervals among subsets of cases otherwise treated alike within the design. (In effect, it crosses a time variable with the other experimental conditions.) These are some additional and unintended temporal windows through which extraneous factors can affect study results.

There is no need to discuss the other true experiment design types or most of the **quasi-experimental design** types in similar detail. Suffice it to say that each of them adds some further complexity of time orders and intervals. Later in this chapter, however, we will discuss some features of the interrupted time series quasi-experimental designs because they exemplify some important points about how temporal issues can be dealt with effectively in study designs. We turn now to a discussion of how the temporal intervals within any design can be regarded as specifications of causal process times.

Time Intervals as Causal Process Times

We need to be concerned with the temporal order of events and the time intervals they entail not only because they represent temporal windows for the operation of extraneous processes but also because they represent durations that reflect the operation of the (suspected) causal processes. If causal processes take time, and if there cannot be causal action at a temporal distance, then to explain the experimental versus control group differential in the flow of causal events between the premeasurement and the postmeasurement of the effect, we need to explore these time intervals as well as their order.

If we intend to make inferences about causal processes that are operating between the purported cause and effect, we need to pick the time intervals we impose within our study design—between pre- and postobservations, between preobservation and the imposition of the experimental treatment, and between treatment and postobservations—just as carefully as we pick the concepts that are to be studied and the values of those concepts that are to be reflected in our experimental treatments.

Specifically, we need to find a treatment-to-posttest time interval that is long enough to allow:

(a) just enough time for the causal processes to operate to their fullest;
(b) but not so much time that some of it is empty of the operation of the causal processes;
(c) and not so much time that some other system forces have begun to operate so as to counter the causal forces under study;
(d) and finally, not so much time that the effects of the cause will have begun to wane.

Using Time-Series Designs to Study Cyclical System Processes

All of these factors are of concern even if the causal processes involved produce monotonic and linear effects, as most of our theories assume. If the effect is actually cyclical, however (or nonlinear and nonmonotonic in other forms), then none of the designs discussed thus far—and indeed, none of the true experimental designs outlined by Campbell and Stanley—would be adequate to assess it.

A design that would be adequate to assess a cyclical effect requires not only a very careful theory involving postulates about the time course of the causal process, but also a design that includes measurement of effects on a series of occasions carefully distributed over time.

Such interrupted time-series designs, useful for assessing treatment effects in situations in which a randomly allocated control group is not feasible (Campbell and Stanley refer to these as quasi-experimental designs), can also be adapted to help identify possible cyclicality in causal processes.

Interrupted time-series designs involve a series of observations distributed systematically across a relatively long time span, with an experimental treatment inserted at one or more spots within that series of observations. For example, we might take measures of production in a work organization every week. After five weeks, we might insert an experimental treatment (call it A). Then, after 10 weeks we might remove treatment A (if it were the kind of thing that can be removed), and after five more week we might impose treatment B. We might or might not have a second factory, or a second department of the same factory, from which we gathered production data throughout the same period, but made no interventions.

Taking for granted for the moment that many other design requirements are met, with such a design we could identify a cause/effect relation even if it were cyclical in time—provided the cycle's interval was not smaller than a week, not longer than half the duration of the study (or, the duration of treatment A or treatment B), and not highly irregular in its variations.

But, of course, the very design complexity that makes it possible to identify and study such complex processes also opens the door (or, in our terminology thus far, opens a temporal window) for many other potential design threats to enter. Furthermore, if the time interval involved in our observations is based on administrative convenience (e.g., production records once a week) rather than on logical or theoretical considerations related to the system processes being studied, even the complex and sophisticated forms of design will not help much in specifying the time course of the causal processes involved. (If we had cyclical trends in productivity, as postulated in the above example, they certainly are as likely to occur day to day, or over months or seasons, as to occur on a week-to-week basis.)

Using Longitudinal Designs to Study Social Change

One form of such time-series designs is called **longitudinal designs.** Many social scientists, especially those interested in studying social change, have called for more use of such longitudinal studies to assess long run effects. But they too have some major weaknesses (e.g., Kulka, 1982).

Complex designs involving combinations of longitudinal and cross-sectional comparisons are needed to separate out the historical (secular), the maturational (developmental), and the generational (cohort) effects that are all inevitably involved in the operation of long run social change processes. (The use of cohort and other longitudinal designs is discussed again in the last chapter of this book.)

Within the study of social change there is the further problem of assessing stability and change over time both in the substantive variables of interest and in the instruments by which they will be measured. In most data-gathering situations, substantive change and **unreliability of measures** are quite intertwined and difficult to separate. The investigator must assume that one of them is not operating in order to assess the other. As is the case for trying to unconfound history, development, and generational effects within change data, the very procedures that can help separate out effects of substantive change from effects of unreliability of measures (e.g., complex time-series designs) infuse still other temporal problems into the matter. (This topic—separating substantive change and reliability of measures—is dealt with again in the next chapter.)

TEMPORAL FACTORS IN THREATS TO
INTERNAL VALIDITY OF STUDY FINDINGS

Earlier, we mentioned that strong designs often use extra comparison groups in order to rule out the effects of intervening events (other than the experimental treatments) that might have occurred between pretest and posttest observations. Campbell and colleagues (Campbell & Stanley, 1966; Cook & Campbell, 1979) call these potential intervening events threats to internal validity, and have identified seven major classes of them: **history, maturation, testing** (or **reactivity**), **instrument decay** (or, more generally, instrument change), **regression to the mean, selection,** and **mortality.** All seven of these are profoundly temporal in character and may arise from temporal problems in the study design. Six of them—all except regression to the mean—vary as a function of the length of the X-Y interval. Some of their temporal aspects are discussed in this section.

History

History refers to potential effects on the actor's (participant's) behavior that arise from events that could occur between pretest and posttest besides the deliberate experimental treatment(s) of the study. Such outside events can produce an effect like the one being studied, or can obscure the observation of such an effect. As the interval between treatment and post observation increases, so does the opportunity for the operation of such outside events.

History effects could arise between pretest and treatment, as well as between treatment and posttest. Such events could arise in the environment surrounding the whole study, or just in the environment of the experimental group (Cook and Campbell refer to the latter case as being local history and as having its effects in the form of an interaction of history and experimental treatment). The more experimental and control conditions the study contains, the more opportunities there are for such differential effects of history.

Consider the following story as a hypothetical example of history effects (mainly in the form of history-treatment interactions):

A research study is planned to assess the educational and attitudinal effects of computer aided instruction in third-grade math. During the summer, next fall's third graders in one school are randomly allocated to one of two classrooms: Lynn Brown's class, which will receive the experimental treatment; and Leslie Jones's class, which will receive the standard third grade math curriculum.

After these assignments were made, but before school started, there was a legal controversy in the community that led to considerable local publicity about the health hazards of use of computer monitors. Shortly after classes began, parents of many of the children in Brown's class forced a meeting with school personnel on the use of computers in the third-grade math class. Although most of the parents agreed to leave their children in Brown's class, all of this drew much attention to the computers—over and above their intended role in math instruction. One would expect, therefore, that there would be an increase in the variability of attitudes toward computers among members of the experimental group at an early stage in the study.

Meanwhile, all of the fuss about computers came to the attention of parents of Jones's students as well. Furthermore, the school's very lavish defense of the educational value of computers was not lost on those parents. Later in the term, they too forced a meeting with school personnel at which they demanded equal educational resources for their children. To mollify them, yet still let the experiment continue, the school agreed to give those children computer aided instruction in language studies instead of in math. This had some effect on the variability of attitudes of Jones's class toward math, but an even greater (but negative) effect on their math performance—because those kids spent much more time than they otherwise would have on language studies and concomitantly less time on math.

These effects are local history effects—interactions of features external to the study design with features of the experimental treatments. Although the example is hypothetical, it depicts relatively frequent kinds of unintended effects within research. Obviously, the longer the temporal intervals involved, the more room there is for such differential effects to operate.

Maturation

Maturation refers to changes within the actors themselves, changes that occur during time intervals within the study that are independent of the occurrence of the experimental treatment. These internal events, developments within the social systems under study (e.g., individuals, groups, organizations), also can either enhance, obscure, or display a spurious form of the cause/effect relation under study. Here, too, as more time passes (between pretest and posttest), more maturational change takes place. Maturational changes, however, need not (and are not likely to) show monotonic increases, let alone linear ones, with increased passage of time. They are likely to reflect developmental cycles.

Testing and Reactivity

Testing effects refer to changes that occur in an actor's behavior because the process of measurement itself sensitizes the actor to his or her own behavior. It denotes effects at the end of the measurement interval that were unintentionally produced by the initial measurement. For example, a questionnaire on attitudes toward air pollution may sensitize the respondent to relevant news stories about air pollution. The more general term, *reactivity,* is used here to denote not just the unintended effects of the measurement process, but also such unintended and artifactual effects of experimental treatments and other features of study procedures.

The time interval between premeasure and postmeasure can interact with such reactivity effects, in any of several ways. As the time interval increases, the sensitization resulting from testing may increase, or may fade. But even if fading takes place, making reactivity a less plausible rival hypothesis, waiting longer is not an unmixed blessing. To increase that temporal interval opens wider the window of time through which history, maturational, and other effects may enter. Moreover, the intended effects of the experimental treatment, the study of which is the underlying purpose of all of this activity, may also fade during such an extended time interval.

Instrument Change

Campbell and Stanley's (1966) term, *instrument decay,* or the more general term, *instrument change,* refers to the effects that ensue when a measurement device changes calibration during the data collection period. For physical instruments (e.g., mechanical or electronic devices), long time intervals of use increase the *likelihood* that parts will break or wear out or rust. For human instruments (e.g., observers, raters, interviewers), either short but full intervals, or long intervals whether full or empty, may have adverse affects on consistency of instrument performance: Fatigue, boredom, forgetting, new learning, and above all, shifts in motivation, all may undercut the reliability and validity of human judgments involved in research measurements. Moreover, these do not necessarily operate as monotonic increases with the passage of time. At first, observers learn, hence improve; later they get bored and fatigued, and the quality of the data they generate decreases.

Selection

Selection is a threat to validity that arises because the fundamental experimental principle of randomization has been ignored. Selection refers to the assignment of actors to treatment conditions on any basis other than random allocation from a common pool. This often occurs when intact groups are selected for study out of convenience or because of their availability. Group differences based on selection (old versus young, male versus female, poor versus rich, etc.) are often (mistakenly) used as if they were the same as a manipulated experimental treatment. But a selection-based treatment cannot be used with a random allocation of cases to levels of that factor. (For example, you can't assign cases at random to be in the old and young groups, or in the male and female conditions.) Therefore, when two batches of cases differ on a selection basis, they likely will differ in many ways not related to the variables that the researcher intends as the experimental treatments; and such differences may be confounded with and mistaken for the causal effects of those intended treatments. Selection involves an indirect temporal effect, in that longer time intervals imply longer times during which any selection-related factors can operate to make comparison groups noncomparable.

Mortality

Mortality or subject attrition refers to effects that can accrue when some of the actors who participated at the first measurement drop out of the study before the final measurement takes place. This may affect the distribution of characteristics differentially for the treatment groups— that is, it may undo the effects achieved by random allocation. Attrition also may interact with the treatment itself, making the interpretative problem more serious. When a study extends beyond a single session there is likely to be some attrition. The longer it extends (both in number of waves of observations or treatment sessions and in total calendar time from start of the study until its completion), the more attrition there is likely to be. So the scope of the problem is directly linked to time, and the seriousness of the problem depends on sampling, design, measurement, and other considerations.

Regression to the Mean

Regression to the mean refers to shifts in distributions of scores of subjects, selected into groups on the basis of extreme pretest scores, when they are subsequently retested on a measure of the same attribute. It is a statistical artifact, not a logical one. If you select subsamples of extreme scores (say a group of "highs" and a group of "lows") on an initial set of observations, the scores of those cases on the average will show a regression from more extreme scores on that first set of observations to more moderate scores on a second set of observations. (The regression works backwards as well as forward in time. That is, if you select two sets of extreme post scores, those cases will show, on the average, much more moderate prescores.)

There is no basis for assuming that the size of a pure regression effect is associated with the duration of interval between the two measurements. The regression effect refers to variations in random components affecting the attribute score as measured. It is the only one of these seven classes of threats to internal validity that does not vary with length of the X-Y interval.

Concluding Comments

Most of these classes of threats to internal validity, that is, threats to sound causal interpretation of experimental results, contain crucial temporal features and can be aggravated by temporal features of the study design. There is considerable empirical evidence, as well as a strong logical case, that the correlation between two measures that are not taken simultaneously decreases as the interval between their measurements increases. For instance: High school rank or ACT scores in high school senior year predict college freshman grades much better than they predict college senior grades. In terms of the discussion in this chapter, the larger the temporal window, the more likely it is that extraneous factors will effect the relation between an earlier and a later measure. The trick, for the investigator, is to arrange the temporal order relations and intervals, among comparison groups and measurement occasions, so as to maximize the chances that you can detect the hypothesized effect (if it is present), and discern the shape of the processes underlying it, while at the same time minimizing the threats to a valid interpretation of that effect as having arisen from the hypothesized cause.

TEMPORAL FACTORS IN EXTERNAL VALIDITY

Part of the meaning of external validity of findings has to do with their generalizability over time, both in the sense of repeated occasions and in the sense of duration of calendar time. Social science researchers have given far too little attention to all aspects of the external validity of findings, and have given scant attention indeed to the temporal aspects of those external validity issues.

Many researchers seem to operate under the assumption that any one period of time is qualitatively the same as any other. This may be a shaky assumption on a number of levels. Phenomenologically, most people (at least some of the time!) do not experience time as a smooth linear flow of undifferentiated moments. Rather, they experience time as **epochal** and as **phasic** in its flow. Different points in time and different periods of time seem to be qualitatively different from one another (McGrath & Kelly, 1986).

At another level, human life is filled with cycles and rhythms, from diurnal cycles of activity and temperature variations to seasonal cycles that bring with them variations in human activities, moods and interests as well as differences in weather. At still another level, there are life stage variations and generational differences that alter both activities and attitudes. It is clear that we need to take into account these nonhomogeneous features of time as experienced if we hope to understand how the substantive phenomena of our field are or are not stable and generalizable over time.

People born in different periods of historical time have different experiences because of different cultural and world events. Such cohort differences, which sometimes are also generational differences, can be viewed in any of several ways. Some investigators have capitalized on those differences as the route by which social change can be studied. Others have interpreted those differences as evidence of instability of our substantive findings over time, hence as evidence of our inability to establish lawful and universal relations among concepts of interest in our studies. This argument seems to assume (incorrectly, we think) that lawful is synonymous with eternal. Nevertheless, we need to make generalization over time a keystone within our efforts to establish the external validity of our research findings.

Up until now, such an emphasis on generalization over time has certainly not been a central feature of efforts toward establishing external validity. There has been surprisingly little effort devoted to external validity in any case, and most of that effort has focussed on generalization over populations. Here, as in other aspects of our field (and of our culture) we have tended to treat time as a "merely": merely a medium within which events take place; merely a dimension of the space-time continuum; merely an abstract parameter that we can use to locate and track people and events; and the like.

Such cavalier treatment of such an important facet of human experience is misleading. It is rather like saying that we should not bother to study human individuals because they are merely the location of certain consequences; merely the agents of many sorts of actions; merely the sources of most of the important stimulation; merely the carriers of the technological and social institutions of the culture. Although that set of statements about individuals might be literally true from some conceptual perspective, just as the statements about time are, to headline each of them with the pejorative *merely* is certainly misleading in both cases.

CONCLUDING COMMENTS

Perhaps one reason why investigators have given time so little attention, either as a substantive variable or in our efforts to establish the external validity of our findings is, ironically, because people in our culture tend to value time so highly—hence to be impatient, to be in a hurry. To study generational effects in a way that separates out historical, developmental, and cohort effects, takes at least several generations. To do cross-sectional comparisons across generations takes much less time. To study static conditions is easier still, in part because it is quicker. *To study time takes time.* And, in our culture, time is scarce, hence valuable, hence not to be wasted.

Both the pervasiveness of temporal features and our neglect of them holds not only for the relatively macrolevel aspects of method that we have considered thus far (e.g., strategy, study design) but also for more microlevel aspects (e.g., manipulation and measurement of variables) as well. The focus of the next chapter is on temporal factors at that operational level.

3

Temporal Issues in the Conduct of Research

Temporal factors also pervade the research methodology of the behavioral and social sciences at the operational level. Time is a crucial part of the methods used to measure, manipulate, and control variables in those studies. Time is crucial to the logic used to assess the quality (i.e., reliability and validity) of data. Many independent variable manipulations involve temporal order or interval. Many dependent variables are measured in terms of temporal parameters, such as **frequency, rate**, and **duration**. And many of those measures involve temporal features in their measurement (e.g., leads, lags) that are critical in their interpretation. But here, too, behavioral and social science researchers have given temporal matters much less attention than their importance would seem to merit. This chapter will note some of the most important temporal issues at the operational level and draw out some of the implications of inattention to them.

TIME, CHANGE, AND THE QUALITY OF DATA

Chapter 1 discussed how social and behavioral science researchers try to strengthen many aspects of their logic of method by leaning on strong assumptions about both the stability over time of the phenomena that they study, and the linearity of change over time in those phenomena. Such assumptions about time also underlie the logic by which the quality (that is, the reliability and validity) of measures and concepts is assessed. This section presents a discussion of those assumptions, with regard to time and measurement.

Factors Underlying Apparent Change

The search for knowledge generally involves a search for differences. In experimental situations, these differences often involve change between two sets of measurements. Whenever two measures of the same attribute or phenomenon are taken on the same cases but at different points in time, the agreement or nonagreement (i.e., the degree of correlation) between those two measures inevitably confounds contributions from at least four sources:

(a) real change in the phenomenon being measured, as compared to invariance, over the time interval involved;
(b) fluctuations of the phenomenon over time that are stable patterned oscillations of the value of the attribute (i.e., recurrent cycles);
(c) systematic differences in the two measurements owing to instrument change or change in the subjects of study, even though the phenomenon itself is stable.
(d) unreliability (i.e., random variations, or error of measurement). (See glossary for **measurement error, reliability of measures.**)

Those four sources of variance are always confounded when one simply measures the same property twice, for the same population, at two different times.

In the preceding chapter, we discussed studies showing a decrease in the correlation between nonsimultaneous measures of two attributes as the magnitude of the temporal interval between their measurements increased. That same principle holds in general for the correlations discussed here, involving two measures of the same attribute. The larger the time lag between the two measures, the lower the degree of agreement (i.e., correlation) between them is likely to be. Such an increased time interval between the two measures would be expected to yield increases in the contributions of both factor (a) (real change) and factor (c) (instrument change) as time between the measures increased. With just two sets of observations, however, there is no good way to untangle the contributions of those factors, (a) and (c). There is no reason to expect the contribution of factor (b), stable oscillatory patterns, to increase with an increase in the time interval between the measures. Factor (b)'s contribution depends more on the timing of the measures in relation to the **periodicity** and regularity of the oscillations. And factor (d), random error of measurement, is uncorrelated with time interval (or with anything else), by definition, since it is random.

Parenthetically, both real change and instrument error probably contribute to most cases in which there is a decrease in predictive power as a function of time lag between predictor and criterion. Such a case was noted in the preceding chapter: The demonstrated drop in the effectiveness of high school rank as a predictor of freshman versus senior college grades. The longer the temporal interval between measures, the more time there is for real change in students' relative performance and abilities (i.e., their learning). It also allows more time for the entry of extraneous factors (e.g., changes in motivation, random opportunities and calamities, shifts in calibration of the measurement instruments, grade inflation), and a longer time for their operation.

Techniques to partly uncouple these two sources of variation—factors (a) and (c), real change and instrument error—involve use of multiple measurement occasions, multiple methods for measuring the attributes, and measurement of different but related attributes as well (Campbell & Fiske, 1959). Some of these are discussed in the final chapter of this book, in relation to longitudinal studies, cohort designs, and time-series designs. None of them is wholly effective in unconfounding the two factors; but use of several in combination can at least attenuate the problem.

Imposing Linearity on Cyclic Processes

None of the techniques just listed, that offer ways to partially unconfound change and measurement error, will in any way help identify and remove, much less focus on and study, variation resulting from factor (b): patterns of oscillation that are stable/recurrent over time. Yet, there is considerable evidence that much human behavior is characterized by such stable patterns of oscillation over time—that it is cyclical, or rhythmic. (See, for example, McGrath & Kelly, 1986; Moore-Ede, Sulzman, & Fuller, 1982; Warner, 1984.) But the core of the logic of method in the social and behavioral sciences, as well as virtually the entire array of methodological tools, is based on the assumptions that true scores (without measurement error) are either stable over time, or change linearly over time when change does occur.

So, for example, when social and behavioral scientists compare the amount of change between two experimental trials (call them trials a and b) that were a certain temporal distance apart, with the amount of change between two other trials (trials c and d) that were temporally much further apart, they tend to expect proportionality in amount of change and amount of time. That is, they tend to assume that the relative amount of change in measures will reflect, directly, the size of the temporal interval.

It is *as if* researchers expect time to map isomorphically to all other measurement scales, and as if they expect the ratio (or interval) properties that are assumed to hold for the time measure to somehow rub off on those other measures. Proportionality would be the case only if all change processes acted in a smooth, monotonic, and nearly linear fashion. As indicated above, though, many behavioral processes seem to operate in cyclical, or oscillatory, or rhythmic fashion. Such patterns violate the assumptions of the interpretive logic underlying typical change comparisons.

In fact, the study of such stable but nonstatic phenomena—phenomena that show stable recurrent cyclical patterns over time—is one area of methodology that has been even less adequately developed than has been the study of change per se. Most social and behavioral scientists seem to have a natural tendency, when faced with repeated measures from a number of successive trials or observation intervals, to add and average the data across those trials. This is done to obtain quantities that are regarded as more stable or reliable estimates of the true score for each attribute. To add and average across trials averages away minor fluctuations. This treats those variations as error of measurement, on the assumption that the properties have true scores that are constant—at least over such short intervals.

But if much human behavior is characterized by stable cyclical or rhythmic patterns (and the evidence to that effect seems very strong indeed), then such averaging procedures, rather than averaging away minor fluctuations that are random errors of measurement, serves to eliminate or mask the very pattern of stable, recurrent oscillation that ought to be a focus of research. Such averaging shows stability within short time intervals—in fact, it can show nothing else but stability if a single measure of central tendency is used to represent all the scores of that interval. But it will mask the actual stable pattern—a cycle or oscillation of some form—and thereby produce misleading interpretations.

Consider an example from a domain with relatively well established measurement techniques—human body temperature. We all know that the average or normal body temperature is supposed to be 98.6 degrees Fahrenheit. Nevertheless, researchers who study **circadian rhythms** also know that most organisms show substantial within-day fluctuations of surface body temperature (and somewhat smaller ones for core body temperature). Those fluctuations trace a smooth cycle across the hours of the day, peaking in late afternoon and evenings, then falling to a low point in the early morning hours. For any given individual, those cycles have much day-to-day stability; they peak and trough at the same times day after day, and at about the same absolute temperature level (ceteris paribus). There is some predictable between-individual variation in those cycles. A systematic within-cycle temporal range of several degrees Fahrenheit is by no means unusual or abnormal.

Note that there really is an average temperature for humans— probably something pretty close to 98.6 degrees. If a series of measurements of body temperature was gathered—say, every two minutes for 15 days, on each of 100 people—they likely would show some value very close to 98.6 as the average for the total set of scores, for the set of scores for each individual, for the set of scores for each day, and for the set of scores for each individual-by-day. But if instead the data were aggregated over individuals for each period of the day, they would probably produce a very smooth aggregate *cycle* (reflecting the circadian rhythm of temperature) in spite of individual fluctuations in cycle peaks and troughs. It is not that an average temperature of 98.6 is not in itself true. It is just that it does not tell the whole story.

What then should a nurse or a parent conclude if a patient or a child shows an oral temperature of 101 degrees at 3 p.m., or if another shows a temperature of 94.4 degrees at 2 a.m.? If the nurse or parent took the 98.6 norm seriously, they might regard either or both of those cases as showing body temperatures aberrant enough to warrant close attention. But if they took the circadian rhythm of temperature seriously, they might find that, for each person's cycle, the measured temperatures were exactly at their average for that time of day. (Conversely, a temperature of 101 at 2 a.m., or a temperature of 94.4 at 3 p.m., might well be indicative of aberrations in the functioning of body temperature regulatory mechanisms. For most people, such temperature values would be way off from the average for those times of day.)

As with the nurse or parent, the researcher really needs more information than just the average score on phenomena of interest in order to understand the meaning of either stability or change in those phenomena. The researcher needs to know the recurring patterns of oscillation over time (if there are any), as well as changes in average level over time (if there are any), in order to construe, sensibly, the underlying logical-causal and chronological processes.

The Validity of Reliability Studies

The concept of reliability, per se, involves a crucial temporal feature. The underlying logic of reliability is that we *compare two simultaneous but experimentally independent applications of the same measuring instrument to the same objects or phenomena to be measured.* This is, of course, impossible to realize in practice. So, all methods for assessing the reliability of measures proceed by relaxing one or another of the constraints in that definition.

Some—such as test-retest procedures—set aside the simultaneity assumption, and try in various ways to wrestle with the experimentally independent assumption. Others—such as alternate forms and split half procedures—keep the simultaneity assumption but set aside the assumption that it is the very same instrument that is being used in the two independent measurements.

The test-retest approach assumes: (1) that the true score of the variable being measured (factor a) either is constant over time or changes uniformly over time; (2) that there are no systematic cyclic patterns (factor b) or that both tests are given at the same point in the cycles; and (3) that instrument changes also are constant or uniform (factor c). Therefore, the extent to which the first and the second measurements do not correlate reflects the unreliability (random variation) of the measure of the variable (i.e., factor d).

Note that many of the threats to validity that we have already discussed—history, maturation, reactivity effects, and the like—may operate within the interval between the two testing applications. The shorter the time between test and retest, the more testing or reactivity effects may come into play. Hence, the shorter the interval between the two testing occasions, the less tenable is the assumption that the two measurements were experimentally independent. On the other hand, the longer the interval between the two testing occasions, the more room there is (i.e., the wider the temporal window) for the operation of such other factors as history, maturation and the like, that can pose threats to the "internal validity of the reliability assessment" activities.

We put internal validity in quotation marks in the preceding sentence to make a point. A set of research operations used to try to establish the reliability of a test or other measure is in fact an instance of a research study design. It is curious that in the social and behavioral science literature reliability testing studies are seldom discussed as involving study designs, and as therefore being potentially vulnerable to all of the threats to internal validity that beset other study designs.

Reliability studies often make use of very weak forms of study design. They are seldom true experiments; they are often preexperimental designs; they frequently do not include relevant comparison groups. What is more, the sampling procedures and the procedures for allocating cases to conditions (if there are any comparison conditions) are seldom made explicit, and are often lacking the crucial random component.

TEMPORAL FACTORS IN STUDY PROCEDURES

Time and Experimental Treatments

Manipulations of independent variables, putative causes, often involve temporal parameters directly. Sometimes frequency, rate, or duration of stimulus are critical features of the independent variable. Sometimes manipulations involve anticipation intervals, warning times, and the like. The study procedures within which the manipulanda are embedded also often contain some critical temporal features: sequence of stimuli, order of presentation of conditions, and the like.

Although every experiment deals with and in some way resolves all of these temporal issues, they are seldom regarded as important method-ological matters. They are most often resolved on the basis of convention, standardization, or counterbalancing. But many of these time-based features of experimental manipulations reflect important assumptions about the nature of the phenomena being studied, and carry important consequences for the information contained in the study.

Arrangements of such temporal features of manipulanda and study procedures are usually built on the assumption that either the behavioral processes of interest are constant over time or that change in them over time is not only monotonic but linear. Researchers often seem to assume that the processes somehow involve ratio scales with respect to time (e.g., that doubling the duration of the presentation of a stimulus corresponds to twice as much of the process).

Furthermore, decisions about the temporal unit of analysis, about intervals within the experimental procedures, and about order relations among conditions are most often made on the basis of convention. If a certain length of working time was used for a task in past research, that same task time will most likely be used in the future for the same task. Similarly, if an effect was found in a previous study after a 15-minute delay, then a 15-minute delay will probably be the only interval used in a subsequent study of the same effect, even though there is no substantive rationale for that interval.

Standardization is an important principle of good research design, to be sure. But standardization is only one of a number of important principles, some conflicting with one another. The exclusive use of the *same* procedures in successive studies of a phenomenon has some serious strategic consequences for our knowledge of that phenomena. McGrath, Martin, and Kulka (1982) argue, for example, that following identical standardized procedures in all studies on a given topic has the effect of limiting the potential information gain of each study. We should note further that, more often than not, these conventional choices—in regard to temporal factors among many other aspects of study procedures—were made in the first instance arbitrarily, mainly for the convenience of fitting into an experimental hour. It is clear why such studies yield little information bearing on the temporal course of causal processes.

Another time-related principle of good experimentation that also has some negative side effects is counterbalancing the order of presentation of stimuli or conditions. For example, if participants are supposed to respond to two questionnaires, A and B, the experimenter may counterbalance the order of presentation such that half of the participants complete questionnaire A first and B second, whereas the other half of the participants complete questionnaire B first and A second. Although counterbalancing prevents such order relations from being confounded with the stimulus conditions under study, at the same time it sometimes prevents investigation of some potentially interesting and important features of the phenomena under study. And, as noted in the preceding chapter, it sometimes creates new temporal windows, within conditions, into which extraneous factors can enter and have unintended effects on the phenomena under study.

One reason why temporal factors are so pervasive in experimental treatments may be the strong influence that logical positivism and behaviorism have had within psychology and other social and behavioral sciences. Time is a very measurable property of events. Furthermore, using objective or clock time does not seem to require any metaphysical analysis or the postulating of any theoretical concepts. Behaviorists not only make use of rates and frequencies in their experimental treatments, but also consider the distribution of events within intervals as important. Fixed and variable reinforcement ratios, and the use of interval or ratio reinforcement schedules, are all part of the standard set of operational definitions of many behavioristic studies. For instance, a fixed-interval reinforcement schedule means that a reinforcement will be delivered after a fixed period of time has elapsed from the last reinforcement, whereas a fixed-ratio reinforcement schedule means that a reinforcement will be delivered after a fixed number of responses are obtained. All of these, of course, are temporal concepts. Further, each type of reinforcement schedule is associated with different patterns of response over time. For example: Fixed-interval reinforcement schedules lead to scallop-shaped response patterns over time (because the participant stops responding for a time after each reinforcement, and then responds rapidly as the time for the next reinforcer approaches). Fixed-ratio reinforcement schedules lead to near step-function response patterns over time (because a high rate of responding occurs after the delivery of each reinforcement). The behaviorists' emphasis on temporal features of manipulanda carries over to their use of temporal measures as dependent variables, as will be discussed in the next part of this section. But the behaviorists' sophisticated use of temporal features of experimental treatments is not widely shared by social and behavioral scientists working out of other research traditions.

Time and Experimental Effects

Many of our measures of effects also contain important temporal features. Here, too, there is a strong influence of the behaviorists, again probably in large part because of the ease of making time measurements and the extent to which such temporal measures appear not to have any problems of reliability, validity and the like. Time measures are almost always regarded as purely objective. Many dependent variables involve rates or frequencies of responding, latencies, or reaction times, and so forth.

Rate or frequency is a record of the number of some kind of occurrence per some predetermined unit of time. What such measures ignore is the distribution of events throughout the interval. It is perhaps no accident that some of the most robust findings in our field are the behaviorists' relations between reinforcement schedules and cumulative strength and pattern of response in relation to learning, extinction and other processes. Those latter findings do take into account the distribution of events (e.g., reinforcements) within the intervals of concern.

Measures of temporal duration also have been used to assess a wide range of variables in social psychological research. Duration refers to the temporal interval between the onset and the cessation of some event. Time durations are relatively easy to assess, and equipment to measure them accurately, even for extremely small time units (e.g., milliseconds), is portable and easily concealed. Most people wear watches, and the sight of someone checking his or her timepiece does not necessarily arouse undue suspicion. Thus, durations can be measured unobtrusively, with high accuracy, and without disturbing the events taking place. (See Webb, Campbell, Schwartz, Sechrest, & Grove, 1981.)

However straightforward time scores may be, methodologically, they pose some serious conceptual problems. The same duration can be used to make different, and sometimes contradictory, inferences about system processes. Time durations have been used to assess the amount of cognitive processing involved in certain tasks (e.g., reaction times in cognitive tasks). Duration of attention, often measured by gaze, has been used as a generalized measure of preference by which to assess the degree of interest in or attraction to certain objects, products, or other people. Following that view, the time spent working on a task has been used as a measure of intrinsic interest in the task. Yet, time taken to complete a task has also been used to indicate the intrinsic interest of a distracting stimulus. Furthermore, time to complete a task has been used as an index of ability or motivation of the actor, and as an index of difficulty of the task. In a similar vein, duration of mutual gaze has been used both as an indicator of interpersonal attraction, and as an indicator of truthfulness or trustworthiness in a speaker.

These uses of duration of some behavior (e.g., staring at a picture or an object, staring at another person, working on a problem) operates as if observation of overt behavior were a direct, monotonic, and linear reflection of either the magnitude or the duration of some internal process (e.g., positive attitude toward the object, positive attitude toward the person, cognitive processing time). Such uses involve some very strong assumptions both about the isomorphism of behaviors and internal states and about the monotonicity of external and internal processes with respect to temporal intervals. In our view, researchers in the social and behavioral sciences need to give more thought and attention to these issues than has been done to date.

TEMPORAL FEATURES OF CLASSES OF MEASURES

Many measures have special temporal properties or constraints directly involved in their use. These need to be reckoned with in the interpretation of findings based on those measures, hence they need to be taken into account in research planning. Too often, they are overlooked.

For example: In stress research, one class of measures, generally accepted as useful indices of reaction to some stressor are on-line, real-time physiological measures, such as the **galvanic skin response** (GSR), pulse rate, respiratory rate and the like. These tend to be labile measures, requiring the establishment of baseline levels and the readjustment of running levels of the measuring instrument for adaptations during extended periods of data collection. In the interpretation of such measures, specific values at specific short periods of time are usually credited to specific stimuli or conditions occurring immediately prior to the moment of measurement.

In contrast, another group of measures, also usually regarded as good measures of reaction to stressors, are those derived from assessment of the levels of various constituents of blood and urine (e.g., accretion levels of sugar, cholesterol, CO_2, and adrenaline products). These cannot be done on-line. Rather, the researcher must wait a substantial time (hours) after the putative causal events in order for the constituents of interest to build up to measurable levels. On the one hand, these measures avoid some of the data quality problems associated with labile measures (such as GSR) that are observed on-line in real time. They yield indices that are much less labile, ephemeral, and transitory than the GSR type measures. But at the same time, these measures do not permit isolation of the effects of any one stress event; rather, they assess the net effects of all events that occurred within the time period of the study.

Still a third class of measures often used in stress research are self reports—instruments such as adjective checklists, questionnaires, and rating scales. These are virtually time independent, with respect to their administration. That is, they can be administered at any time before, during, or after a stressful event. They are most often used in retrospect, either immediately or after a delay. They can even be used in anticipation of hypothetical stress events that will never be experienced. This enormous temporal flexibility is paid for at a high cost in reactivity, and in other potential threats to validity.

Suppose you obtained a battery of measures of stress effects, containing some of each of these classes (e.g., GSR, a blood sample, and a self-report), and then asked the triangulation or convergent validity question of them, namely: How well do the measures correlate with each other and to what extent do they give the same answer to the question being examined? It is likely that these different measures of reaction to stressors would show little convergence, simply because of their diversity on temporal characteristics—quite apart from the question of whether or not any one of them is a valid measure of stress (or the even more fundamental question of whether stress is a valid and useful concept) (McGrath, 1981). The measures would probably not correlate highly with each other. Each one shows a characteristic pattern of variation over time quite apart from the operation of some stressor causal process, X. No one level of temporal aggregation would make sense for all three of them. The time-sensitive GSR would likely show a highly labile pattern of variability, moment to moment, whether or not that pattern also showed systematic increase (or decrease) over longer intervals of time. Various constituents of the blood sample would show only substantial differences over a substantial period of time—likely, a number of hours or more. It would not be sensible—and perhaps not possible—to compute minute-by-minute scores on components of the blood or urine. As for the self report measure: It would be hard to administer a questionnaire on a minute-by-minute basis, and to do so would certainly court reactivity. A questionnaire could be used to ask respondents to say, retrospectively, how they had felt minute by minute, but those responses would hardly be regarded as highly independent answers. In any case, there would be no reason to expect such a timeless measure as the questionnaire to correlate highly with either the relatively stable blood constituents or the highly labile GSR. Such a lack of correlation would be so even if each of the measures was a highly reliable measure of a valid and useful construct.

These problems extend far beyond stress research. Indeed, certain temporal features are characteristic of various classes of measures. We will review some of those temporal characteristics here, using the four types of measures (**self-report, observational, trace,** and **archival**) described by Webb and his colleagues (Webb et al., 1981) to do so.

Self-Report Measures

Self-reports are extremely versatile with respect to time. They can be used during important research events, immediately after them, after either a short or a long delay, in anticipation of such events in the future, or in relation to hypothetical events that never do occur. But that very temporal flexibility is also temporal indefiniteness, which brings with it serious threats to the validity of findings based on such measures.

First, a short time interval between event and measurement courts reactivity effects, since the participant is likely to have good memory for the event and may be more likely to try to discern an experiment-appropriate response. On the other hand, a long interval courts effects from faulty or biased memory of the event. And as in the discussion of study design in an earlier chapter, the longer the time interval between the experimental event and the measure of it, the larger the **temporal window** through which extraneous factors can enter and bias results. For example, if positive life circumstances had occurred between a stressful event and the assessment of the amount of stress in the event, those positive circumstances might bias the participant's responses in a positive way.

Selection of self-report measures as a main form of assessment, then, poses the researcher a dilemma, which can be resolved only by an unsatisfactory trade-off between high temporal flexibility (or indefiniteness) and potential problems involving reactivity, instrument change, and other potential threats to validity. The other classes of measures pose equally troublesome, though complementary, choices.

Observational Measures

On-line observations may avoid some of the problems of self-reports in regard to temporal interval, but they do so at a high cost in personnel, equipment, and training effort to obtain high quality data in an inherently labile situation. The GSR is an example of such observation using a physical instrument. Content codings of communication behavior in a group is an example of such observations by a human instrument.

We noted earlier that records of GSR responses show extreme lability, and the instrument's running level must be recalibrated frequently during a trial to retain its value in indicating variations in relative response. In a sense, this is typical of all on-line observations taken in relatively microscopic temporal units. For communication in a group, for example, there is high variability in regard to the sounds being uttered (the who, what, and why of them) at any subsecond instant of a group problem-solving activity—even though there might be a great deal of patterned consistency in records of such work groups if they are viewed at a larger temporal level, such as a minute or a quarter hour or the total task work time. Indeed, communication within a group often shows stable oscillatory patterns over time—factor b in the earlier discussion of change—as well as both change over time (factor a) and variations owing to instrument change (factor c). But, at least, the on-line nature of direct observations, which allows collection of temporally fine-grained series of measurements, closes the temporal window through which numerous extraneous factors might otherwise have entered.

The meaning of any such observation is closely coupled to the specific events immediately preceding it. In this sense, single on-line observations are very particularistic (and appropriately so, since that is the nature of the flow of behavior). To aggregate those into more stable, hence more reliable, indices, is to average away whatever evidence they might hold regarding stable cyclical or oscillatory patterns (factor b). Furthermore, such aggregated measures will have meaning only in relation to all the events within those larger segments of time over which the measures were aggregated. They will have lost their temporally fine-grained potential—one of the main advantages of observation. As with many other aspects of methodology, choices regarding temporal aspects of measures involve dilemmas that cannot be resolved in entirely satisfactory ways.

Trace Measures

Trace measures are, by definition, accretions, or erosions made by the behavior itself unbeknownst to the actors involved. Examples include hormone deposits in blood samples, the wear and tear on tile around museum exhibits, and trampled grass on the most used paths across a field. These measures avoid the problems of reactivity, since the actor is unaware of the measure of his or her behavior. But they are at the same time entirely opaque with respect to the several time intervals involved in their generation, acquisition, and use: The time processes involved in the laying down of the traces, the time interval over which the various traces to be recorded were accumulated, the time since the traces to be recorded had all been laid down, and so forth. Furthermore, their meaning is not at all tied to particular events. Rather, they are aggregations that accumulate deposits of various phenomena over relatively long periods of time (as, for example, with the blood and urine constituents). Hence, they can be interpreted only in relation to all the events within relatively long time intervals.

Archival Records

We did not include any instances of archival records in the earlier example from stress research, but there are many such examples that could be used. For instance: Stress research sometimes makes use of records of past visits to health facilities, or days absent from work for sickness. Such information often can be obtained from company records. The behavior underlying each archival measure is presumably recorded without research reactivity, because it is not at that time intended for use in research. But it may nevertheless suffer from what might be called *administrative reactivity*. That term refers to distortions in what is recorded, and how it is recorded, as a function of ongoing forces (political, economic, social, personal) in the system the behavior of which is being examined. For example, for reasons having to do with work standards and production norms, production records are sometimes reported to management in ways that, though accurate over a longer period of time, are shown as smoother day by day than was actually the case. Threats of such potential selective recording, as well as of selective survival, and differential distortion, increase as the length of either of two time intervals increases: (1) the time over which the data

were recorded in the first instance; and (2) the time between that
recording and current use. Archival records are also likely to be
recorded in temporal units that reflect administrative convenience in
recording, rather than natural units of system process. It is sometimes
hard to translate these time intervals into intervals that are meaningful
reflections of causal or system process times.

Concluding Comments

All classes of measures tend to have characteristic, and differing,
temporal signatures. Sensible interpretation of data resulting from their
use requires that these be taken into account. Archival records often
have long time frames, and so do trace measures; observations often are
temporally fragile, so to speak; self-reports are apparently time-flexible
but actually time-indefinite, and in any case are subject to reactivity and
other threats to validity that operate in the temporal window between
experimental events.

TIME AND THE CONDUCT OF RESEARCH STUDIES

We have already noted three ways that time plays a part in our
research at the operational level: (1) Temporal parameters are much
used in experimental manipulations; (2) frequencies and response time
measures are often used as indications of cognitive and behavioral
processes; and (3) many dependent variable measures involve time-
sensitive features. Beyond these three sets of temporal effects, temporal
features are pervasive, though broadly neglected, within many aspects
of study procedures.

Researchers who study human behavior are accustomed to designing
studies that somehow handle all major factors that might affect results,
even when those factors are not of interest in the study. Such a factor can
be handled in any of a few ways: by controlling it at the same value for all
cases in the study (and reporting that value in the methods section); by
counterbalancing it with respect to experimental conditions (and
reporting those procedures); by randomly allocating cases, hence, by
randomly allocating variations of that particular factor across conditions of the study; or by allowing the factor to vary freely, measuring it,
and then regarding it as a potential covariate of the variables of interest

(i.e., to be subjected to statistical control rather than experimental control). (See glossary for **control, control group, counterbalance, randomization.**)

It is considered good experimental practice to use and report such control procedures with respect to as many potentially relevant extraneous factors as possible. Sometimes studies report having used one or another of those four techniques to control such factors as: size of the cardboard or paper on which stimulus materials are printed, color of the walls in the experimental rooms, makes and models of experimental equipment. One would think that some of the various temporal factors discussed here would be regarded as at least as likely to affect results as those kinds of features of the study situation.

Yet, an examination of our journal literature makes it very clear that social psychologists almost never even make reference to time of day, day of week, season of year—much less any more particularized temporal information—at which any of their cases were observed. They seldom mention keeping any of those time intervals constant across subjects. They seldom mention counterbalancing cases with respect to any of those times.

In fact, in a sample of all of the articles in one recent year of a leading journal, we found that virtually none of the studies indicated any information about any of these times. (For all we know, all of that data was collected at 2 a.m. on Christmas Eve, hence vulnerable to a visions of sugar plums effect!) In fact, in most of those studies (at least 90%) we don't even know from the report how long the experiment took for a given participant, or whether it was the same or different for different cases. Since most of the studies in that year-long sample were experiments in which a participant was involved in only one session, few of those studies provided any information about calendar time between sessions for different participants. Few of them provided any information about clock time between experimental events within the single session. The time order of events, however, is reported religiously.

These types of temporal information can sometimes be extremely important in interpreting the results of a study. For instance, a finding of higher factory productivity after some experimental intervention might be interpreted quite differently if it was assessed during a time of high seasonal productivity (such as before Christmas) rather than during a more moderate seasonal trend. That is, the effect might have occurred at that time of year regardless of whether or not there was an intervention. As another example, in a study on teacher effectiveness as measured by the attention level of the students, one would expect to find very different results for assessments made during 8 a.m. classes and those made during 11 a.m. classes.

Perhaps investigators don't report temporal information about their studies because they are confident that there are no such seasonal or diurnal effects, and assume that the reader will trust them not to neglect important factors while omitting unimportant ones (including some of the temporal factors discussed here). But one would think they might make the same assumption about their reader's trust vis-à-vis stimulus size and lighting in the room and the brand of electronic equipment used. Yet there is a strong tendency—apparently a very widely shared norm—to report such physical variables, but to ignore temporal ones.

If the message of this and previous chapters has been heard, then researchers should more carefully report about the time-structure of their treatments and observations, at least in as much detail as they do about the physical arrangements within which their experimental activities occur or the physical properties of their experimental materials or the detailed wording of their experimental instructions or interview protocols. Experimental reports should include information that tells the reader whether various time referents and intervals: (a) were held constant across participants (and if so, at what values), (b) were measured and used as covariates (and if so, whether they did in fact covary with the behavioral processes of interest), (c) were counterbalanced among participants with respect to study conditions, or (d) simply were ignored. Reports should indicate, for each case, when data were collected from that participating social unit in each observational wave. The reader needs enough information to be able to relate those times of observation (for any one participant, and among them) to clock and calendar events (was it at night, was it on a weekend, how many minutes did the session last, etc.), and to features of the institutional setting (was it during midterm week, was it the first day of classes after vacation, was it payday, was it on a Friday afternoon).

Beyond these clock and institutional times, it is probably unreasonable to expect that most studies gather individualized information about the myriad personal time frames (e.g., developmental cycles, civil, economic, and social events in the person's life). To do so, however, is certainly called for in field studies designed to reflect behavior under natural conditions. Such information is generally a feature of case studies, adding much to the richness—but also to the cost—of those studies.

When described in detail, the collection and reporting of such data seems like an inordinate burden on the researcher, especially when the researcher has no interest in the variables involved (and, as in the apocryphal story with which we began this book, time is not a theoretically interesting variable!).

But the actual operational burden is much less than meets the eye. In most studies, the time location of any experimental activity is a datum that is automatically available to the investigator, veritably begging to be collected. Furthermore, time data can be obtained in a form that is relatively free of reactivity factors, rater reliability problems, or the like. The investigator almost always knows exactly when each participant was administered a certain questionnaire, and can easily record exactly when that participant finished it. We always know (or easily can know) at what time of day, what day of week, what time of year, and what place in the institution's work cycle, each such treatment or measurement activity takes place for each participant.

If time offers such potentially important data (as we believe it does), and if it is so free and easy to obtain, it is even more remarkable how systematic social and behavioral science researchers have apparently been in avoiding the collection of time information in empirical research. It is a situation similar to what seems to hold for information about gender of participants. That information, too, is more or less automatically available; yet it is also systematically underreported in the research literature of the social and behavioral sciences. We think both of those oversights, however unwitting, are unacceptable practices for the future.

Keeping and reporting such a record of times that each experimental event (treatment or observation) occurred for each case is necessary to let the reader assess the effectiveness of experimental procedures (counterbalancing, control, etc.) with regard to those temporal variables— the topic of this section. It is also a necessary part of the temporal structure needed at the study design level if we are going to explore any of the temporal factors thus far discussed. That latter aim is dealt with in the last two chapters of this book.

CONCLUDING COMMENTS

The temporal features of method discussed here, and many others, are crucial features of the research process. They cannot be wished away. They can be, and often are, ignored, but not without cost. As in other instances in which serious methodological issues are ignored, those issues often become our undoing in myriad subtle ways. So it is currently, we believe, in regard to temporal factors in many areas of social and behavioral science.

The question is: What can be done about such temporal issues? How can we incorporate features into our research procedures to take into account these temporal matters? That topic is the focus of the remainder of the book.

4

Exploring the X-Y Interval: Some Tactics for the Time Structuring of Study Procedures

In the first three chapters of this book we focused on raising issues about the role of temporal factors in research in the social and behavioral sciences. In the last two chapters we will describe some techniques and practices that can help researchers deal with some of those temporal issues.

Note that we are not offering solutions to those temporal problems. There are no solutions, as such, for most of them. Rather, these temporal issues, for the most part, do not pose solvable problems, but unresolvable dilemmas that are part of the fabric of the research enterprise itself. What we offer here, therefore, are guides for incorporating those issues into study planning so as to anticipate and perhaps offset some of their consequences. This chapter deals with issues at the level of study procedures. The next chapter deals with issues at the level of research strategy and study design.

This chapter focuses on the **X-Y interval**: The time between occurrence of the putative cause, X, and observation of the outcome variable(s) of interest, Y. In the first section, we consider how one can plan study procedures to explore X-Y (that is, cause/effect) relations of various temporal shapes. The outcome variable under study, Y, may track any of a number of temporal forms, even when it is not subjected to any experimental treatment: It may be constant over time, it may change linearly over time, it may show a nonmonotonic form, it may be cyclic, and so on. The causal variable, X, also may have any of several temporal shapes: it may be a one-shot event, it may be either a continuing or an accumulative effect, it may be recurrent, and so on. The first section of the chapter describes these various temporal forms of X and of Y.

The second section considers putting these X and Y shapes together to generate an ordered hierarchy of potential temporal patterns for any X-Y effect. These include a difference between conditions that happen to be time ordered, a one-step increase (or decrease) over time, a change in slope; recurrent oscillations (i.e., cycles), and changes in phase or periodicity of cyclic processes. Detecting them requires data sets that are progressively more elaborate and temporally more structured. In the second section, therefore, we consider the minimal requirements of data to detect evidence of each kind of temporal effect. That section also notes some mathematical and statistical tools that can help in this effort, and cites a number of sources in which those techniques are applied to interesting social and behavioral science issues.

That discussion is followed by consideration of a third topic: The recognition that things other than the effect of X can also occur within the X-Y interval. This discussion first considers the X-Y interval as a temporal window through which factors reflecting a number of plausible rival hypotheses can enter. Then it considers the possibility that processes or events within the substantive system, that are not themselves the focus of study, may influence the behavior processes that are being studied—thus misleading the investigator as to the impact of experimental events and experimental intervals.

These considerations lead us to a final topic of the section: The need to somehow reconcile two divergent time scales: real time or system time (i.e., the time orders and intervals involved as processes get played out in the substantive system under natural conditions), and experimental time (i.e., the time orders and intervals, and other time relations, internal to the methodology of a given study design). This reconciliation needs to be done in terms of a conceptualization of the system that deals effectively with its dynamic, temporal features—a **conceptual time**. Then, in order to construct an experimental time plan that somehow jibes with both the conceptual time and substantive system time, we need a theory of **temporal scale** that lets us translate effectively among the three: system time, conceptual time, and experimental time.

That last point—concern for arranging studies so that they have the kind of conceptual structure that permits proper exploration of the temporal facets of the field—brings us to the point at which this chapter ends and the following one begins. In the chapter to follow, we will talk about some ways to establish a temporal structure on our overall study plans—a temporal template. In that chapter, we will be dealing with temporal structure at the more macrolevel of research strategy and study design; whereas in the present chapter our discussion is focused at the more micro level of manipulations, measures, and other study procedures, dealing with a specific X-Y interval.

THE X-Y INTERVAL AS BOTH LOGICAL AND TEMPORAL RELATION

The statement, X, then Y, is both a logical and a chronological statement. As noted in Chapter 1, it refers to both a causal and a temporal order relation and to three kinds of intervals. Beyond the requirement that there be a fixed order—X must precede Y—the social and behavioral sciences have given little attention to the fit between the causal and temporal features of the X-Y relations that they study.

Most study designs in social and behavioral science research imply that the delivered increment of X will yield a fixed increment of Y—and that variations in the duration of the X-Y interval will neither add to nor diminish that increment. According to this view: Y exists at a certain level. The treatment, X, is applied. Y moves to a higher level, and stays there.

Other study designs imply that the duration of X-Y—the time from when X is turned on until Y is measured—will map to the magnitude of the increase in Y; that is, that the magnitude of Y will increase as a linear function of time between application of X and measurement of Y. Few researchers posit hypotheses—much less design studies—that would explore nonmonotonic relations between the duration of the X-Y interval (the temporal relation) and the magnitude of the increment in Y that is expected or observed (the causal relation).

There are a number of reasons why we ought not assume either that the effect of X on Y is static with respect to time, or that the X-Y relation produces a uniform linear change over time in Y. Some of these reasons have to do with features of the process, Y; some have to do with features of the causal agent, X; some have to do with the features of the X-Y combination.

Temporal Shapes of the Outcome Process, Y

In Chapter 1, we discussed a number of patterns that an outcome variable, Y, can show over time. In that discussion, we assumed that some experimental treatment, X, was being imposed on a process, Y, and that Y was in a more or less static condition until X came along. But the system process represented by the outcome variable, Y, may itself show any of several patterns over time, even when it is not modified by the action of putative cause, X.

First, it may be a stable, unchanging process that reacts, when perturbed, by reestablishing equilibrium. Second, it may increase over time (as in the growth of an organism). Such increase might be, but need not be, linear. Indeed, the process represented by Y in its undisturbed state (that is, without intervention of X) need not even be monotonic over time. Many important biological and behavioral processes reflect endogenous rhythms or oscillations or cycles (McGrath & Kelly, 1986; Moore-Ede et al., 1982; Warner, 1984). So when an experimenter imposes an experimental treatment, X, that intervention is always done in a context in which the system process, Y, is itself already playing out some temporal shape over time.

Temporal Shapes of the Causal Agent X

Not only does the outcome variable, Y, have some shape over time, the causal agent, X, can also vary in several ways that affect the temporal course of the X-Y relation. (See Figure 4.1.) From this temporal point of view, Xs can be of any of at least four basic kinds:

The one-shot agent: Such Xs are delivered as a single discrete event, not left on and not repeated (see Figure 4.1a). An example would be use of some presession instructions to experimental subjects.

The continuing condition: Such Xs are turned on and left on, to deliver a continuing and constant level of the treatment until turned off—as when a fan is turned on and set to deliver a constant wind speed (see Figure 4.1b). An example from the social and behavioral sciences would be assigning participants to a certain kind of task condition for a continuing series of trials.

The accumulating condition: Such Xs are turned on and left on, to deliver the treatment with cumulative impact—as when water is allowed

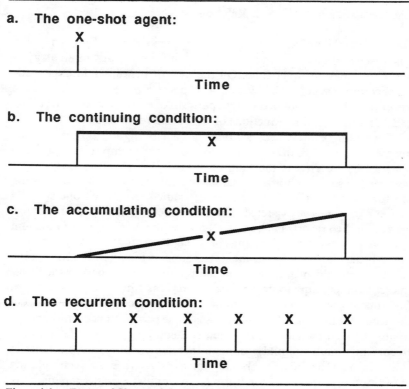

a. The one-shot agent:

b. The continuing condition:

c. The accumulating condition:

d. The recurrent condition:

Figure 4.1   Temporal Shapes of the Causal Agent X

to flow into buckets of a water wheel, with the accumulating weight of the water leading to action (Y) (see Figure 4.1c). An example from the social and behavioral science area might be the cumulative effects of some stressor variable (such as noise), as it continues to be in the on state. (It is worth noting that the investigator often cannot distinguish, a priori, between causes that produce continuing effects and those that produce cumulative effects.)

The recurrent condition: Such Xs get delivered repeatedly, at some predetermined periodicity (see Figure 4.1d). An example would be the presentation of a new stimulus item (or reinforcer) every n seconds.

Temporal Shape of the X-Y Relation

In principle, an experiment could impose any of the four types of X just discussed on a system process, Y, that followed any of an array of possible functions over time. On the face of it, we would expect the application of Xs of each of the above types to Y processes of each of the several forms, to result in different patterns of increments in Y over time (that is, different time functions of the causal relation, X-Y).

For example, an X that is a one-shot agent might produce a single, unchanging change in Y—if Y followed a static temporal form in the absence of X. That is the kind of change that so often seems to be assumed in social and behavioral science study designs. But, depending on the nature of the Y process being studied, even such one-shot Xs might sometimes be expected to deliver either: (a) a momentary change in Y, that then reverts back to pre-X levels (as when Y is an equilibrium seeking process); or (b) a change in Y that then continues to increase—linearly or otherwise. Experimental treatments that deliver a continuing stimulus should produce a continuing effect on Y, perhaps a linear increase or perhaps some diminishing returns function. Experimental treatments that deliver an accumulating stimulus condition should yield an accumulating effect on Y—perhaps some power function rather than a simple linear increase. Finally, experimental treatments that deliver a recurrent stimulus should produce either a series of spikes or a series of steps in Y. Certainly we should not expect either an accumulating condition or a recurrent condition to deliver just a single step increase, persistent or not.

In any case, we certainly should not assume in advance that a given application of X will have an impact on Y that is a constant amount regardless of time, or that the magnitude of the effect of X on Y will be a linear function of the X-Y interval.

These ideas have serious implications for study designs. To explore relations of any shape more complex than the linear case—or even to test the assumption of a linear relation—requires that we observe Y at multiple times. At least three waves of observations are needed to assess linearity; four or more observation waves are needed to explore nonmonotonic forms or cycles. Social and behavioral science studies seldom have more than two such waves.

GAINING INFORMATION ABOUT THE X-Y RELATION

A Temporal Hierarchy of Effects

There is a hierarchy of levels of information about potential time related effects, and these are tied to different degrees of temporal fine-grainedness of observations.

Static designs. The first level of information is what can be obtained from a static design—measurement of some behavior on a batch of social units on a single occasion. Such a data set potentially contains useful descriptive information about that occasion, but it contains no time related information at all.

Change in level designs. The next level of information is what can be obtained from designs in which the investigator observes, then imposes a treatment, then observes a second time. In the terminology popularized by Campbell and his colleagues (Campbell & Stanley, 1966), this is the classic O-X-O design, whether or not it has control comparisons, O-X'-O, and whether or not cases are randomly allocated within it. In the terminology used here, it is a $Y_1 X Y_2$ design. In such a design, we hope to be able to identify a change in level that is associated with the logical order ($Y_1 X Y_2$). That logical order is, more or less coincidentally, confounded with the time order ($Y_1 X Y_2$). The difference in level, between Y_1 and Y_2, is usually much more appropriately regarded as a difference owing to the condition, X, than as a difference owing to the passage of time per se. In fact, strong forms of such designs often include a comparison group of randomly allocated cases that received $Y_1 X' Y_2$, in order to show that time alone (or, more accurately, the effects of history, maturation, or other plausible rival hypotheses associated with the passage of time) did not produce the posited difference.

Monotonic change designs. The next level of information can come from designs that have sets of observations from three points in time. What follows assumes that, if the study in question is an experiment, all but one of the observation occasions occurred after the critical experimental event (i.e., $Y_1 X Y_2 Y_3$). Whereas designs at the first temporal level (static designs) can show only one pattern (the mean of the observations for that occasion is whatever it is), and designs at the second temporal level (change of level designs) can show three patterns (Y_1 is higher than Y_2, or lower, or the same), designs at temporal level three, which we will call monotonic change designs, can show five different patterns of outcome all of which involve interesting interpretations. Assuming we have one experimental treatment and three waves of observations, as Y_1, X, Y_2, Y_3, then:

(a) The three means for the three occasions can be the same (i.e., stability).

(b) The mean can rise from time one to time two, then retain that level (or, conversely, go down and retain that level): a permanent change in level.

(c) The mean can rise from time one to time two, and rise further at time three (or conversely, fall, then fall further): a monotonic, perhaps linear, change.

(d) The mean can stay the same from time one to time two, but then rise at time three (or fall): a change with a lag or delay.

(e) The mean can rise from time one to time two, then fall again at time three (or conversely, fall then rise): a temporary change, though a hint of an incipient cycle.

Nonmonotonic change designs. Designs at temporal level four—Y_1, X, Y_2, Y_3, Y_4—which we will call *nonmonotonic change designs,* can yield six different patterns of means. Five of them permit us either to have greater confidence in, or to disconfirm (depending on the lie of the final point), the kinds of patterns already noted for the lower levels— stability, temporary change, and so on. The sixth is a potential pattern that can be seen only at this level and above:

(a) The four means on the four occasions can be the same (i.e., stability, which we can regard more confidently as such);

(b) The mean can rise from time one to time two, then retain that level at times three and four (i.e., a permanent change in level, about which permanence we can be more confident);

(c) The mean can rise from time one to time two, and rise further at time three and again at time four (or fall and continue to fall): a monotonic change, the linearity of which we can more confidently assess.

(d) The mean can stay the same from time one to time two, then rise from time two to time three and retain that level at time four or, similarly, remain at the first level through three observations, then rise at time four (or do the same in the downward direction): a change in level with a lag or delay.

(e) The mean can rise from time one to time two, then fall again at time three and stay down at time four or, similarly, stay up at time three but fall again at time four (or do the same in the downward direction): a temporary change, less likely to be a cycle.

(f) The mean can rise from time one to time two, then fall at time three, then rise again at time four: an irregular and nonmonotonic effect, suggesting a cycle.

Cycle detection designs. It is only at temporal level five—Y_1, X, Y_2, Y_3, Y_4, Y_5—that one can detect a cycle with some confidence, and then only if the cycle is no longer than two observation intervals. We will call these *cycle detection designs.* At level five there are still six basic interpretable patterns. Each of the first five (as above) can be further confirmed with one more point that fits the interpreted pattern (stability, monotonic/linear change, etc.), or its pattern can be disconfirmed by the final point. But the sixth form—up from time one to time two, then down at time three, then up at time four, and down again at time five—can clearly denote a cyclical pattern—or, of course, can disconfirm the cyclic pattern suggested in the first four points if the fifth point does not lie where the cycle would project it.

Observation interval and observation period. It is important to remember that the preceding statements about number of waves of observation needed to study cycles represent a minimum and fits only when the observation interval is more or less exactly half the cycle period. What is specified here is the minimum number of waves of observation that is *logically* necessary to detect a cycle if present (and if the data had no error of measurement). What is necessary for statistical detection of cycles under conditions of fallible measurement is much, much more demanding. But even for the minimum logical case, in general, detection of cyclic processes requires a series of observations at least long enough to span twice the duration of the periodicity of the cycle. On the other hand, if the cyclic processes involve times shorter than the between-occasion interval, they will be missed altogether. For example, assume that there is a one-hour performance cycle that ebbs on the half hour and peaks on the hour. If performance is observed only once an hour, that cycle could not be detected. (The observations would be the same from one observation to the next; the magnitude would depend on when within the hour the observations were made.) The more fine-grained the set of observation intervals and data analysis intervals, the more readily cycles can be detected if they are present. In principle, one can detect cycles at any periodicity from twice the size of the minimum between-occasion interval up to half the time duration of the total string of observations. You can't detect cycles shorter than your most fine-grained interval.

But cost goes up rapidly with replications of observation occasions. So time intervals must be chosen carefully in relation to the processes studied. For example, some prior thought needs to be given to whether cycles of certain periods, if present, would be of special interest for theoretical reasons. The logic of cycles is not the same as the logic of mean differences, or even the logic of linear (or monotonic) trends. In short, you need a conceptual time plan to help construct your methodological time plan, in order to study the substantive time processes of the systems of interest. This theme will be brought up again in the final section of this chapter.

Most social science studies collect data on only one occasion, or at the most on two occasions. Very few studies collect data from three, four, or five occasions. So one can hardly argue that such research has not "found" cycles in past studies. Rather, those past studies have systematically avoided looking for cycles. Furthermore, most studies that have gathered observations on multiple ordered occasions have then computed averages over those successive trials, and thus averaged away evidence of oscillatory processes as though they reflected error. Thus, even when measures have been collected from multiple occasions, typical study plans have virtually guaranteed that the body of evidence will stress static or change-in-level processes.

Thus, there is a "vicious cycle of neglect" of temporal effects in substantive, conceptual, and methodological domains of the field. Cyclic processes (and any other complex temporal processes) have been systematically excluded from the empirical evidence of past studies, as described above, by getting few waves of observations and by averaging away variations over time. This has led to a parallel systematic exclusion of complex temporal processes from conceptual systems of the field: If we don't find cycles empirically, we don't need to build hypotheses about them. This, in turn, has led to the almost exclusive use of study designs that are relatively low in the temporal hierarchy we have been discussing. And use of such designs will continue to guarantee that no such temporal processes will show up in the empirical evidence of subsequent studies. It is vital, we believe, that social and behavioral science research break out of this dysfunctional cycle of atemporality.

Some Mathematical and
Statistical Tools That Can Help

There are some methodological and statistical tools for analysis of complex temporal patterns, and a considerable increase in such tools in recent years. These can help break that cycle of neglect of temporal processes. Although a detailed presentation of these tools is beyond the scope and purpose of this book, in the next few pages we will discuss several specific areas in which such developments seem to be promising for the study of temporal processes. That brief discussion will not provide a detailed treatment of any of the methods discussed. Rather, it will highlight possibilities, and provide a guide to some more detailed presentations of those methodological tools.

For many purposes, **spectral analyses** and **Fourier transform analyses** are the methods of choice for searching for cyclic patterns. They are mathematical and statistical procedures designed to identify any recurrent regularities (i.e., cycles) within a time-ordered series of observations, and to specify the frequency or periodicity of each pattern (i.e., the frequency of each cycle). Although these methods have been used much more in fields other than the social and behavioral sciences, nevertheless social and behavioral science applications of these are described in a number of fairly recent books and journal articles, among them: Dabbs (1983), Gottman (1979), Porges et al. (1980), and Warner (1984).

Spectral analyses are designed to identify cycles within a series of scores on a given variable (i.e., the set of successive observations Y_1, Y_2, Y_3, and so on). These methods are powerful. They will identify all of the cycles in a set of observations, within the set of criteria and constraints that are used in a given data analysis application. These constraints include the frequencies selected for testing, the temporal patterning of the data itself, the criteria for identifying presence of a cycle at a given periodicity, and the like. But like all powerful statistical and mathematical tools, their use requires very strong assumptions and some stringent conditions for the data. Use of these methods requires a long series of observation occasions at relatively small time intervals, with the intervals between successive waves of observation equal (or assumed to be equal). The techniques will identify (or at least work best with) only patterns of relatively uniform recurrence—wave forms that are symmetrical about the baseline on both axes (such as sine waves). Of course, even with those stringent limitations these methods represent a major advance in our ability to study temporal processes, compared to the static analyses usually applied in social and behavioral science studies.

A related set of techniques, cross-spectral analyses, can be used to search for patterned temporal relations between two or more variables— that is, the effect of one variable (say X) at a given time on another variable (say Y) at a specified later time. Such cross-variable or cross-process influence is implied in the idea of interpersonal influence or dominance; and Gottman (1979) has made use of cross spectral analyses to study patterns of interpersonal dominance in married couples. (Such cross-correlations are discussed further in Chapter 5.)

In addition to the cross-spectral analyses just discussed, there has recently been considerable other work on methods for modeling or analyzing sequential influence processes in dyadic interaction. For examples of such work, see Budescu (1984), Dillon, Madden, and Kumar (1983), Hewes, Planalp, and Streibel (1980), Kraemer and Jacklin (1979), Wampold (1984), and Warner, Kenny, and Stoto (1979). Some of these deal with issues of lagged dominance, or temporal sequences of person to person influence (as does the Gottman work on marital couples, referred to earlier). Some deal with analysis of categorical data, which is especially useful for data generated by interaction observations.

Another set of analysis techniques that are especially useful for studying temporal patterns is the class of mathematical models called **stochastic models**. These techniques model system processes—in the present case, they would be social and psychological processes—over a series of units of time. Stochastic models trace the process under study through a series of instants of time by calculating what the probability is that the system will be in each of its possible system states at time 2, given that the system is in a particular state at time 1, for all starting places. There have been relatively few uses of stochastic models in the social and behavioral sciences thus far. Most of them have used the type of stochastic models called one-step **Markov chain models**. Those models make two very constraining temporal assumptions: First, one-link Markov models make an assumption of **path independence**, namely: that the transition from time i to time j does not depend on anything prior to time i. With this assumption, Markov models need deal only with one-link chains of influence. Second, one-step Markov models make the assumption of **stationarity**, namely: that the probability of a transition from one state to another is the same across time, hence, transitions from any one instant of time to the next can all be treated as interchangeable.

Stochastic models need not impose the strict and constraining temporal assumptions of stationarity and path independence that are included in the most-used one-link Markov chain models. It is possible to develop stochastic models that relax either or both of these two assumptions; and although such models are complex to use, they can be very helpful in studying systems in truly dynamic forms. For recent examples of excellent uses of such models to assess temporal features of some complex social psychological processes see Hewes, Planalp, and Streibel (1980) and Kerr (1981).

Still another body of work that offers considerable promise for the study of temporal aspects of social psychological processes is the elaboration of structural models to incorporate time factors. Structural models are mathematic schema that make use of sets of structural equations to describe the state of a system and the pattern of relations between its parts. Although structural models are, in general, static (as the very name implies), some of them can be used, at least in principle, in a more dynamic way. For example, some structural models have incorporated temporal factors into them by reformulating those temporal factors in a static form. A case in point of such a temporal transformation is in some of the so-called hazard models that are used to model and predict accidents, natural hazards, and other low-frequency events. Such transformations can be put into an even more temporally sensitive form by redefining what event is to be modeled. Rather than trying to model or predict the occurrence of some specific behavior, as is the case with most of our models, these **hazard rate models** attempt to predict the point in time at which a change in behavior or conditions will occur, or the time interval between such changes. An example of such work, emphasizing temporal factors although not dealing with social psychological phenomena, can be found in Birch (1984). Work that adapts and extends such approaches to some interesting social psychological issues (attendance at or absence from work, or from other social action settings) can be found in Harrison (1987).

A further notable advance is in the application of a formal mathematical theory called **catastrophe theory.** It is a formal mathematics for dealing with systems that have multiple stable states and discontinuous functions. Catastrophe theory deals more thoroughly with temporal considerations than have most of our models in the past. It may be especially valuable for some of the more complex forms of temporal processes. A good explication of how such models can be useful for studying temporal issues in our field can be found in Stewart and Peregoy (1983).

This brief discussion of some currently available mathematical and statistical techniques for studying temporal phenomena has three aims. First, it is intended to bring these techniques to the attention of social and behavioral science researchers. Second, it is intended to guide them to literature that will provide further information about those methods. Third, it makes clear that at least some methodological techniques are available that can provide one route for social and behavioral science research to break out of the cycle of neglect of temporal patterns that was described at the end of the preceding part of this section. If social and behavioral scientists begin to plan data collection so as to apply such time-sensitive analysis techniques as those described here, those studies will probably begin to get empirical evidence of temporal processes, and those research efforts will then need to build time factors into their conceptual formulations.

THE X-Y INTERVAL AS A TEMPORAL WINDOW FOR CONFOUNDS

Unfortunately (from the point of view of the behavioral and social science researcher), the operation of the intended effects of X is not the only thing that is going on in the X-Y interval. That X-Y interval is not only a period during which the causal processes under study (the X-Y relation) are running out their course; it is also an interval during which all other factors that are free to vary can be having their effects. This includes two major classes of factors that can confound study results. First, there are a set of extraneous factors that represent classes of plausible rival hypotheses. A number of them—effects of history, maturation, and so on—were discussed earlier in this book. Most of these operate during the X-Y interval. Second, there are a myriad of system processes that can affect the outcome variable, Y, or the X-Y process that is the focus of study. Such system processes can operate as if they were causal factors, experimental treatments. They are pseudo-Xs.

Both extraneous factors, and system processes other than the X-Y relation, must be taken into account. Doing so implies having some systematic picture of the time dynamics of the entire system that is under study—not just the X-Y relation that is the subject of our hypotheses.

More generally, what is needed is some basis for translating among three kinds of time that are operating in the system-as-studied: system time (or real time), experimental time, and a conceptual time in which we formulate the theoretical relations we are studying. Those three issues—the X-Y interval as a window for plausible rival hypotheses; the X-Y interval as the locus for operation of other system processes; and the need for a theory of temporal scale, to translate among system time, experimental time, and conceptual time—are the three topics of this section.

The X-Y Interval as a
Temporal Window for Rival Hypotheses

How long to wait, after X, before measuring Y, is not only a matter of concern because of the importance of the shape and duration of the causal process, already discussed. It is also a matter of concern because the X-Y interval poses an opportunity for the operation of any of a number of threats to the internal validity of a study. Indeed, six of the seven classical Campbell and Stanley (1966) threats to internal validity—history, maturation, selection, testing or reactivity, instrument effects, and mortality—are temporal in character, and operate during the X-Y interval (which in Campbell & Stanley symbols would be the X-O interval).

Reactivity effects have a different relation to that X-Y interval than do all of the others. Presumably, reactivity effects would be at their greatest if the measurement of Y immediately followed the imposition of X, or if it immediately followed a prior measurement of Y. As the time between successive measurements of Y increases, and as the time between the administration of X and the subsequent measurement of Y increases, the likelihood of reactivity effects should diminish.

In contrast, the probability of occurrence of all of the other plausible rival hypotheses or threats to validity (with the exception of regression to the mean) increases as the interval between X and Y increases. In fact, as indicated in an earlier chapter, the X-Y interval can be thought of as a temporal window, through which can slip effects of history, maturation, mortality, selection, and instrument change. The longer the X-Y interval—the "wider" the temporal window—the greater the chances for a condition reflecting one of those rival hypotheses to occur, and the longer the time period for its operation.

So the duration of the X-Y interval is crucial both to minimizing reactivity and to reducing other potential confounds. Furthermore, there is no specifiable solution, by way of a choice of some particular interval, even in a given instance. As is so often the case in the realm of methodology, the choice we face poses not a solvable problem but an unresolvable dilemma: The longer the X-Y interval, the less chance for reactivity effects but the more chance for history, maturation, instrument-change, selection, and mortality effects.

It is important, therefore, for behavioral and social science investigators to design their studies in ways that try to connect the X-Y intervals they use to temporal features that would occur in the systems they are studying under natural operating conditions. The rest of this chapter is concerned with such relations.

The X-Y Interval as Locus for
Operation of Other System Processes

Much human behavior is cyclical or rhythmic. The myriad of circadian rhythms are examples of some, but not all, of the important cyclic processes involved in human behavior. These cycles can range in periodicities, all the way from microsecond on neural and subcellular levels through hourly or daily or monthly activity patterns. Many involve **endogenous rhythmic processes** that do not need any external signals to initiate them, but become mutually synchronized with one another in phase and periodicity. (See glossary for **endogenous rhythm** and **endogenous system processes.**)

It is likely that some of the processes that are of interest in any given social and behavioral science study involve such rhythmic processes, even though research techniques used in that study may not be adequate to assess them. Each such rhythmic process is always operating as part of the system that the researcher is trying to learn about (even when that researcher chooses to ignore it). The timing involved in such a cyclic process—its phase and periodicity, as well as its magnitude—is important both in specifying how that process will unfold and in indicating how it interacts with other system processes.

An experiment entails inserting events into the experimental sequence (i.e., experimental treatments) that, it is hoped, will cause changes in behavioral processes of interest. In effect, the experimenter is implicitly hypothesizing that the experimental treatment will act as if it were an endogenous system process that influences the processes underlying the behaviors to be measured.

Conversely, every event in the substantive system that is capable of acting as a causal agent for the process under study can be regarded as a potential rival experimental treatment—as a shadow treatment the effects of which may mimic, counter, or confound the effects being studied. The time location of any event that might influence the process being studied can be regarded as the location of a kind of shadow treatment, a hidden experimental manipulandum—hidden to the experimenter as well as to the participants. Such events potentially can effect that process—and if they do, they will do so at places within the experimental template at which causal events are not supposed to be happening.

These ways of viewing the study context point up the importance of taking such temporal features of the systems under study carefully into account, even in studies in which the researcher is not interested in those temporal variables.

The Need for a Theory of Temporal Scale

The processes of natural systems unfold according to their own timing and rhythms. Experimental studies of such systems, however, typically strip away that temporal context and replace system time with experimental time. This modus operandi has at least three effects:

(a) It imposes artificial time intervals between X and Y (or between various Xs and various Ys), as has been discussed.

(b) It fails to reinstate some of the system's natural processes—those that the investigator doesn't care to study, or doesn't know about—and therefore leaves out the potential interactive effects of those processes on the X-Y relation.

(c) It reconstructs even the chronological order of some parts of the system—for example, it insures that the variable that is to be treated as a causal X occurs prior to the manifestation of the variable that is to be treated as outcome Y, even if, in nature, both X and Y oscillate continuously and interdependently.

It is one thing to create an artificial experimental context with its experimental time, and study sets of experimenter-driven events occurring in that artificial context—in pursuit of understanding of those abstract processes under pure or "vacuumlike" conditions. It is quite another matter to translate back to patterns of events played out in natural systems operating under system time. Social and behavioral scientists are all aware of this problem in its general, nontemporal form. Our field has only rudimentary theoretical concepts to help translate the meanings of patterns of relations among variables, between the experimental context and the real world systems that they are intended to model. There are absolutely no conceptual tools at all for translating the temporal features of those relations. We need—and do not have—a theory of temporal scale.

Every experimental event—treatment, observation, or unintended experimental artifact—can be represented as at a location in each of several time frames: so-called objective time of the culture's predominant clock and calendar, institutional time, and personal time for each of the study participants. Each such event can also be represented as at some location in experimental time. And the intervals between each such event and subsequent experimental events (e.g., observations) are amounts of time available for the operation of various system processes and of various extraneous factors with potentially confounding effects.

One principle underlying our logic of method, discussed earlier in this book, is that causal processes take finite amounts of time. Another principle is that we cannot have causal action at a temporal distance. Therefore, causal processes must operate within these temporal intervals (the X-Y interval) during which effects are supposed to be generated, and they must fill those intervals. Yet, as we argued earlier in the book, social and behavioral science researchers have given almost no time and thought to the nature of those causal intervals, or to how they might go about establishing or estimating their durations.

Experimental events, and the intervals associated with them, have to do with causal processes that are putatively introduced by the research itself. But the system being studied has a number of endogenous processes that produce effects by operating over time. Many of these operate in cyclical or other nonmonotonic forms. Cyclical processes take a specifiable amount of time to deliver their effects, and if the timing of our observations provides either less time or more time than that specified amount, those processes will fail to show the expected effects.

Any given complex system is apt to contain many such endogenous system processes. These operate independent of any intervention on the researcher's part, and do so whether or not that is convenient for the researcher's study. Indeed, one of the things we try to do in laboratory experiments is to strip away as much as possible of the system's context so that such extraneous system processes will not operate. But although these processes are extraneous to our study, they are indigenous to the systems we are studying, hence they should be at the center of our concern.

We must therefore pay very close attention to the timing of experimental events—treatments, observations, and unintended artifacts—in relation to ongoing system processes in addition to the ones we are interested in studying. But to pay such careful attention to the timing of experimental events, in relation to the temporal operation of a number of system processes beyond the ones the effects of which are of central concern, implies that we have a conceptual formulation of the system itself that is virtually fully developed in its dynamics. Because of our neglect of such temporal considerations, however, we are a long way from having such fully dynamic conceptualizations in most areas of our field. And it is precisely such a dynamic conceptualization that is needed to carry out the task discussed in this section: To map between experimental time and system time in some systematic fashion that lets us anticipate some of consequences of the temporal occurrence and patterning of both experimental events and the system processes underlying them.

In an earlier chapter, we discussed the use of computer simulations as a research strategy. Computer simulations, properly constructed, offer one means by which we can explore dynamic processes within systems and dynamic systems over time. To do any computer simulation, we need to already know (or assume) everything about both the behavioral processes of interest and the surrounding system context within which those processes get played out. To use such simulations in a time-sensitive design means that we must have some way to represent the real-time or system-time intervals within the conceptual model that is the simulation. Those representations are hypotheses about system dynamics; and the computer simulation can let us examine the potential viability of those hypotheses (but not their empirical validity). But within those constraints, computer simulations can be very helpful in our time studies—if only because they force us to attend to, and make postulations about, time intervals we would otherwise ignore.

Computer simulation models that are both dynamic and stochastic are hard to construct and hard to execute (although rapidly increasing availability of high powered computational facilities makes the latter problem one that will be less constraining in the future). In order to construct and run such a simulation, one must specify a large number of assumptions about the operation of the system being modeled—including assumptions about time ordering and intervals of various system events and processes. The intellectual effort required to develop such a simulation of the operation of a dynamic system might turn out to be very much worthwhile—even if one never actually ran that simulation on a computer. That effort can help resolve the problem that lies at the heart of our ability to study temporal effects: The fit between system process times and the timing of experimental arrangements. In short, the development of time-sensitive designs that can be used to explore the dynamics of those substantive systems requires the very kinds of detailed conceptions of the dynamics of systems that a computer simulation forces us to construct.

CONCLUDING COMMENTS

In this chapter, we have urged social and behavioral science researchers to be more sensitive to the temporal assumptions involved in existing methodological practices, and to structure their research to enable them to investigate temporal factors in the phenomena they study. We have emphasized that many processes of interest to behavioral scientists are nonmonotonic in form, hence that study of such processes requires more complex study designs than have ordinarily been used in our fields. We also have stressed that to examine these temporal processes properly requires that researchers plan their observations with respect to the temporal dynamics of the systems they are studying.

It should also be clear that proper time-structured experimentation involves not only the development of methodological techniques, but also the development of conceptual formulations about the temporal nature of these processes. That is, we must have some theory about the temporal course of the processes under investigation, as well as some methods for examining them. The development of temporally structured experimentation goes hand in hand with the development of temporally structured theory, and both are necessary to an understanding of the temporal structure of real world systems.

In this chapter we have focused on the temporal features that are related to a specific X-Y interval. In the chapter to follow, we will try to provide a systematic planning perspective for time-sensitive research—a *temporal template,* so to speak—at the level of an entire study.

5

The S-B-O Template:
A Framework for Study Planning

In the previous chapter we discussed some techniques that can be used to help explore the logical and temporal relations involved in an X-Y interval within a given study. In this chapter, we will discuss the research information that potentially can be adduced from various forms of study plans. The chapter proceeds by laying out a generic framework—a temporal template—within which the investigator can consider any of a number of crucial temporal issues, such as those raised in earlier parts of this book, and plan for reckoning with their consequences. We will refer to the overall schema as the **S-B-O template**. (The basis for its name will become clear as we describe it.) The first three sections of the chapter are devoted to laying out successively more complex portions of the S-B-O template.

Such a template can help plan studies that are more time sensitive. It does not "solve" any of the temporal issues raised in earlier chapters. Nor is it a concrete study plan that could be used to run a specific study. Rather, the template is intended to serve a consciousness-raising device for researchers in the social and behavioral sciences regarding temporal issues. It can help the investigator anticipate consequences of some of the temporal issues, point out where compromises need to be made regarding temporal variables, indicate where temporal issues are being put aside without consideration, highlight where monotonicity and linearity are being assumed with little evidential basis, and so on. Furthermore, such a temporal template may help us see how we can adapt and modify various components of current methodology to make them work in more time-sensitive ways. The final section of the chapter explores three such applications of the S-B-O template—to **autocorrelation**, to **interrupted time-series designs**, and to complex **cohort designs**.

The S-B-O template presented in Figure 5.1 has a number of close conceptual kin within recent social and behavioral science formulations. Notable among these close kin are: (a) the seminal work of Campbell and Fiske (1959) on the multitrait multimethod matrix; (b) later developments and extensions of that schema (e.g., Fiske, 1982; Hammond, Harm, & Grassia, 1986), including parts of our own earlier work (Runkel & McGrath, 1972; McGrath, 1981); (c) Tucker's (1966) landmark work on three-mode factor analysis; (d) methodological schema for exploring causal patterns in correlational data (e.g., Humphreys & Parsons, 1979; Kenny, 1975); and (e) several conceptual frameworks in the specific content areas of personality, emotion, and mood (e.g., Cattell, 1966; Epstein, 1983; Hedges, Jandorf, & Stone, 1985; Larsen, 1988). These formulations all differ from one another in a number of respects, although each emphasizes multidimensional data structures that include a temporal axis. The S-B-O template presented in Figure 5.1 differs from all of them in several respects, notably in its particular focus on the temporal axis of the data structure and on temporal issues in data analysis and interpretation.

PATTERNS OF DATA IN AN S-B-O TEMPLATE

In social and behavioral science research, the basic piece of information, the unit datum, is a record of "somebody doing something, somewhere." Earlier in the book (and in the glossary), we introduced the term *actor-behaving-in-context* (Runkel & McGrath, 1972) to express that idea. But actor must be taken to mean not just an individual, but any of a variety of human agents whose behavior or its consequences is the focus of inquiry—individuals, groups, organizations, and so on. So in this chapter we are going to use the term **social unit** to refer to that human behaving agent. Runkel and McGrath used the term *behaving* to refer to any measurable attribute of the states or actions of the actor or the context. We will use the term **behavior variable** in roughly that same way. Finally, Runkel and McGrath used the term *context* to refer to physical, social, and temporal features of the situation in which the behavior is taking place. Instead of the term context, here we will use the term **occasion**, to emphasize its temporal aspects. So, here we will regard

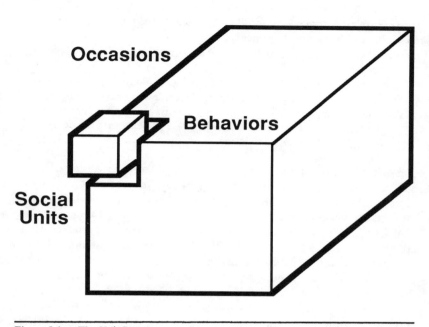

Figure 5.1   The Unit Datum

the basic piece of information, the basic datum, as a record of some social unit (S) behaving (B) on some occasion (O).

Since knowledge is knowledge of differences, a record of a single observation is not yet useful as research information. That observation must be compared with other observations that are in some ways comparable to it, in order to gain information. Hence, the researcher needs to have more than one datum, more than one S-B-O record, before he or she can begin to learn about the events of interest. We will call such a set of observations an **S-B-O array**.

An S-B-O array contains records of multiple observations. These can be drawn from one or more social units (S), one or more behaviors (B), or one or more occasions (O). There are, therefore, a number of different patterns of observations, a number of different types of S-B-O arrays, that an investigator can construct in his or her study. We will describe nine such types: three involving variation on only one of the axes, S, B, or O; three involving variation on two of the axes; and three ways to construct an array involving variation on all three axes.

Research information is about relations between sets of observations. In social and behavioral sciences, those relations are usually expressed as one of two kinds of relations between variables:

(a) a relation expressing *covariation* of the two variables—e.g., when one is high the other is high, and when the first is low the other is low; or

(b) a relation expressing a *difference* on one variable that is accompanied by a difference on the other—e.g., when X is present, then Y occurs, and when X is absent, Y does not occur.

Such relations can be in any of a variety of forms (e.g., covariation can be linear or curvilinear; relations can be in positive or negative directions; relations can be among three or more variables). Furthermore, it is possible to translate, at least conceptually, between covariation and difference relations (i.e., differences are a special case of covariation). For purposes of this chapter, we will use the language of correlation coefficients in our discussions, talking mostly in terms implying covariation between two variables; but we intend that discussion to apply to all of these kinds of relations.

Each of the nine types of S-B-O array contains information about certain patterns of relations among variables but not about other possible patterns. For example, some contain comparative information about more than one social unit, others do not. Therefore each type of S-B-O array contains certain kinds of potential research information and not other kinds; hence, each can be used to answer only certain kinds of questions. Altogether, 18 different potential patterns of relations can be identified within this set of nine types of S-B-O arrays. Many of those 18 patterns of relations involve temporal factors, in one or another of several forms. In the next three sections of this chapter, we will describe each of the nine different types of S-B-O arrays, starting with the simplest forms and proceeding to the more complex, and identify the types of relations between variables that each of those arrays potentially can give us.

PATTERNS OF DATA IN ONE-AXIS S-B-O ARRAYS

The first three types of data patterns to be discussed are the S-B-O arrays for which the observations refer to multiple instances on only one

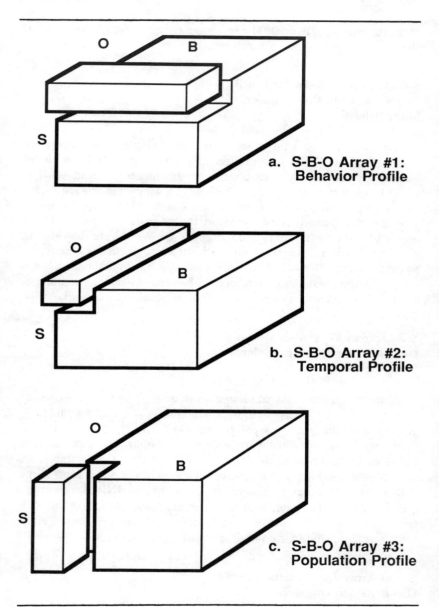

a. S-B-O Array #1:
   Behavior Profile

b. S-B-O Array #2:
   Temporal Profile

c. S-B-O Array #3:
   Population Profile

Figure 5.2   One-Axis Arrays

of the three axes, S, B, or O. They provide straightforward patterns that yield useful, but limited, research information.

S-B-O Array #1: Behavior Profile:
One Social Unit, One Occasion,
Many Behaviors

Suppose you had a lot of test scores on a single person from one testing session. What information could you adduce from them? Basically, you could try to see if there was any pattern in them—that is, which of the tested attributes had high scores, which had low scores, for that person at that time. In other words, you could develop a *behavior profile* of that person on that occasion, for the behaviors involved in or implied by your test battery. For example, we might have that kind of pattern when we are reviewing an applicant's credentials for selection to some position. If the social unit was a work organization, or a community, we would be examining the pattern of behavior in that unit at that time. Such studies are often thought of as *static case studies*.

S-B-O Array #2: Temporal Profile:
One Social Unit, One Behavior,
Many Occasions

Suppose, instead, that you had a score on a single type of behavior repeatedly, over a series of trials or occasions, for a single social unit. Here, you could look for a pattern among the scores on the different occasions—that is, you could develop a *temporal profile* for that behavior by that person over that set of occasions. For example, we would have that kind of data pattern if we listed the population of the state of Montana each year since statehood, or the GNP in each of the past 20 quarters, or an experimental animal's reaction time on each of a series of trials, or someone's grade point average in each of eight semesters. Such data are sometimes called *trend data*.

S-B-O Array #3: Population Profile:
One Behavior, One Occasion,
Many Social Units

Suppose, now, that you had scores on only a single behavior and for only a single occasion, but for a number of different people. We could regard it as a *population profile* on that behavior at that time. For example, suppose you had answers from a whole sample of people on the question: If the election were held today, which of the candidates would you vote for? In other words, you would have a *survey* of that population on that behavior on that occasion.

Concluding Comments

Each of these three types of matrices is useful, but each is extremely limited in what information it can provide. Studies using such one-axis matrices are sometimes referred to as descriptive studies, in contrast to studies that attempt to test hypotheses about relations among two or more variables. These single-axis studies can describe the average and the distribution of scores, and any pattern in that distribution, but the distribution is across only one axis. In one case, that distribution is of scores on different tests or behaviors but for the same person on the same occasion; such studies are sometimes called static case studies. In another case, the distribution is across time, but for a single social unit and a single behavior—hence, it can be regarded as a historical record of that variable for that social unit. The third case deals with a distribution among social units, but for a single behavior and a single time, hence again is just a description of that population on that one variable on that occasion. Ordinarily, none of these permit the investigator to assess covariation or difference relations between variables, although there are some specialized versions of them that do permit calculating such relations within the scores on the single axis of variation. One of these, autocorrelation, is discussed in the final section of this chapter. The cases dealt with next, patterns of data in two-axis arrays, do allow for the examination of covariation relations between variables.

PATTERNS OF DATA IN TWO-AXIS S-B-O ARRAYS

There are three different combinations in which you can vary two of the axes of an S-B-O array. Furthermore, each of those two-axis patterns can be used in either of two different forms (as will be described below), and the two forms of each give two different types of relations between variables, hence two different types of research information.

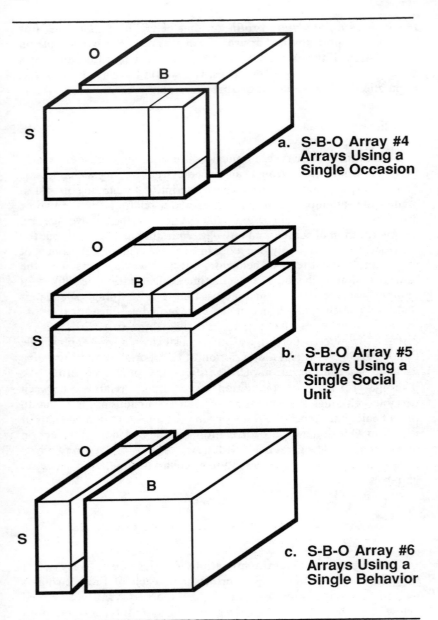

a. S-B-O Array #4
   Arrays Using a
   Single Occasion

b. S-B-O Array #5
   Arrays Using a
   Single Social
   Unit

c. S-B-O Array #6
   Arrays Using a
   Single Behavior

Figure 5.3   Two-Axis Arrays

Therefore, these three S-B-O arrays lead to six types of relations and six patterns of research information.

The three types of two-axis S-B-O arrays are as follows:

For one of them (S-B-O Array #4), you have a number of social units and a number of behavior scores on each, but for only one occasion. This is in many ways our standard research practice.

For a second one (S-B-O array #5), you have a number of behavior scores on each of a number of occasions but for a single social unit. These are sometimes regarded as longitudinal case studies.

For the third (S-B-O Array #6), you have a number of social units and measure them on a number of occasions but only on a single behavior variable. Though these are rather rare, they could be used to search for and compare temporal patterns (e.g., cycles) on a given behavior.

When you set out to do relational analyses on the data of an S-B-O array, you must use distinctions on at least one axis to define variables that you will then relate to one another; and you must use the instances on at least one other axis as the cases across which you will make your comparisons—the "n" over which you calculate correlations or means and variances. Ordinarily, you want to use a large number of instances on the axis you intend to use to provide the n for subsequent correlations. But often you may want to use only two or three or a few instances on the axis that is to provide the definitions of the different variables to be studied. In type #4, for example, you could use a few behaviors and correlate them over a large number of social units, or you could use a few social units and compare their profiles on a lot of behaviors, in both cases for only a single occasion. Similarly, both of the other two-axis arrays, #5 and #6, also can be done in each of two forms. Hence, six types or subtypes of two-axis S-B-O arrays will be listed below.

S-B-O Array #4:
Arrays Using a Single Occasion

As noted, when you collect an array of S-B-O observations that vary on two of the axes, you can use a large number of instances on one of the axes, to provide the n for subsequent correlations, but use only two or three or a few instances on the other axis to provide the definitions of the different variables involved. Thus, there are two forms of a type #4 array. One has only two or three behavior variables but a large number of social units, thereby perhaps testing covariation among all pairs of those behavior variables over that population of social units (for the one occasion). The other type #4 array has only a few social units, but a large number of behavior variables, thereby perhaps comparing the behavior profiles of that set of behaviors between different social units (on the one occasion).

S-B-O Array #4a: (Static) Behavior Relations
One Occasion, Two or a Few Behaviors, Many Social Units

This type of S-B-O array is one of the major data patterns used in studies in the behavioral and social sciences. The study involves only a single occasion. Two or a few behavior variables are measured on a population of respondents—usually individuals. Then, those behavior variables are correlated with one another over the population of social units.

A major variant of this form of study is the case in which one of the variables of interest is experimentally manipulated. For example, a variable, X, may be kept high for one set of social units, and kept low or absent for the other social units in the study. Then that manipulated difference is used as if it were a measured behavior variable, to ask whether each of the other variables (Y_1, Y_2, Y_3, etc.) covaries with the manipulated variable X. That question is usually asked in difference testing terms rather than in correlational terms. (See the discussion of functional interdependence relations in the section on three-axis S-B-O arrays later in this chapter.)

The manipulated form allows more powerful inferences about direction of any covariation pattern found between the manipulated variable X and one or more of the measured variables, Y. Otherwise, this type of S-B-O array for both the straight correlational form and the experimental manipulation form yield much the same kind of research information. Both provide information about the covariation between behavior variables over a population of social units for a single occasion—which we have labeled *Static Behavior Relations*.

S-B-O Array #4b: Comparative Behavior Profiles
One Occasion, Two or a Few Social Units, Many Behaviors

The other form in which a single occasion S-B-O array can be used is to gather a large battery of measures on just a few social units—a few individuals, or a few industrial plants, or a few communities—on a single occasion. This, too, is a rather common pattern of data in behavioral and social sciences. There could be an experimental manipulation variant of it, as well. In that variant, for example, we could conduct a field experiment in which some major behavior variable is modified in one (or a few) social units—for example, a major change in production flow in plant A—but left alone in the other social unit(s). Then, the investigator would search for pattern differences in the other behavior variables between the experimental and control plants. In either the straightforward correlation case, or the field experiment case, the resulting information has to do with differences (or similarities) in the pattern of behavior measures between two (or two sets of) social units. We refer to such relations as *Comparative Behavior Profiles*.

S-B-O Array #5:
Arrays Using a Single Social Unit

As with S-B-O type #4, there are two different ways to use an S-B-O array that has only a single social unit but varies on the other two axes. One of them uses only two or a few behaviors but many occasions; the other uses only a few occasions but many behaviors. The first is about temporal patterns of behaviors; the second is about behavior profiles of different occasions.

S-B-O Array #5a: Behavior Profile Change
One Social Unit, Two or a Few Occasions, Many Behaviors

In S-B-O array #5a, many behavior variables are measured on several occasions, but for only a single social unit. If the social unit were an individual, such a study might be considering the correspondence of a battery of test scores on two or three occasions—how consistent, over time, is this person's test profile, or how does it change. Instead, if the social unit were one department of a work organization, the study might be considering what behavioral features of that plant have changed from one testing time to another. In either case, we can construe these S-B-O arrays as dealing with *Behavior Profile Consistency or Change*.

S-B-O #5b: Temporal Behavior Relations
One Social Unit, Two or a Few Behaviors, Many Occasions

In S-B-O array #5b, the investigator has measures of a few behavior variables on many occasions for a single social unit. If that social unit were an individual, for example, the study might be dealing with measures of several task performance variables of interest (rate, errors, quality of item) on a series of task performance trials. If the social unit were a company, the study might be examining several important production variables (production rate, cost, absenteeism, turnover, new orders, and so on) over a series of monthly periods. In both cases, we would be looking for relations between sets of behaviors over time, for that social unit. We labeled these *Temporal Behavior Relations.*

S-B-O Array #6:
Arrays Using a Single Behavior

For S-B-O array #6, as for the previous two, there are two contrasting ways in which the S-B-O array can be organized. One of them uses two or a few social units, and measures a single behavior variable on many occasions for each of those social units. The other uses two or a few occasions, but measures the behavior for all members of a population of many social units on each of those occasions. The former is about similarities, over time, between social units on that particular behavior. The latter is about reliability of that behavior over time, within a population.

S-B-O Array #6a: Temporal Profile Comparisons
One Behavior, Two or a Few Social Units, Many Occasions

In S-B-O array #6a, a single behavior is measured for a few social units on many occasions. If those social units were individuals, the study might be tracing the time course of that behavior variable for each person, and then comparing the response histories of these different individuals. Much learning research done in the behaviorist tradition is of this form. If the social units were work organizations, or schools, or states, the resulting pattern of data might trace some particular descriptive characteristic of those units over time (e.g., cost per unit produced, unemployment), enabling comparisons of those temporal profiles. We designate them as *Temporal Profile Comparisons.*

S-B-O Array #6b: Reliability Studies
One Behavior, Two or a Few Occasions, Many Social Units

In S-B-O array #6b, a single behavior is measured for a population of social units on each of two or a few occasions. For individual social units, one study might be assessing the time-to-time reliability of some test, or some other performance measure, within that population. For social units at an organizational level, one study might be exploring whether the distribution of that variable in the population of organizations had changed from one period of time to another—for example, do the 50 states continue to have the same relative population sizes (or number of unemployed, or number of college students, or whatever). Note that the same form of relation between variables can be construed as a reliability question, or as a question of substantive change. We designate this pattern of relations as *Reliability Studies*.

Concluding Comments

Although the two-axis S-B-O arrays represent a major increment in complexity over the one-axis patterns, still more elaborate data patterns can be identified if studies generate data that can be represented in three-axis S-B-O arrays. In particular, the data patterns of such three-axis arrays can be used to examine questions of *consistency/change* over time, *convergence/nonconvergence* among behaviors, *similarity/difference* between social units, and *influence/independence* across two of those axes. They are the topic of the next section of this chapter.

PATTERNS OF DATA IN THREE-AXIS S-B-O ARRAYS

A study can be more complete—though more complex—if it gathers observations that make use of more than one social unit, more than one behavior, and more than one occasion. But there are three different ways to organize such a full-fledged, three-axis S-B-O array. As before, each of the arrays requires that there be a relatively large number of different instances of one of the axes, to provide a basis for assessing covariation (that is, enough instances to serve as the n for correlations). But unlike the two-axis cases, the investigator can define the variables to be studied in terms of combinations of two or a few instances of the other two axes. We will identify these three types of S-B-O arrays in terms of the axis that is used as the correlational basis. Thus, we have one type (S-B-O array #7) that uses many social units to explore *population patterns,* another type (S-B-O array #8) that uses many occasions to explore *process patterns,* and a third type (S-B-O array #9) that uses many behaviors to explore *behavior patterns.* However, each

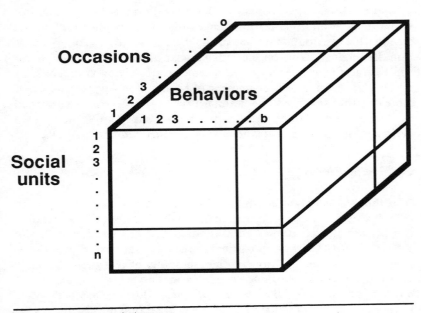

Figure 5.4   Three-Axis Arrays

of these types of arrays generates three different types of relations (correlations), as will be discussed in the following paragraphs. Therefore, a three-axis version of an S-B-O array yields a total of nine different types of research information.

S-B-O Array #7: Population Patterns
Two or a Few Behaviors and Occasions,
Many Social Units

In S-B-O array type #7, the investigator gathers observations about each of several behaviors (B_1, B_2, and so on) on each of several occasions (O_1, O_2, and so on) for a population of many social units ($S_1, S_2, \ldots S_n$). This is another major standard form in which research is done in the social and behavioral sciences. If the social units are a population of individuals, such a study might involve testing questions about whether two or more variables change together within a population. This might be done correlationally, or by means of an experimental manipulation of one of the variables of interest. This array is a temporal extension of S-B-O type #4a, which we called static behavior relations.

This type of array yields three different sets of correlational information (or, more generally, information about covariation).

#7a. One kind of information comes from correlations (across the social units) between two variables that have the same behavior in common but different occasions. (Correlations of B_1O_1 with B_1O_2.) These have to do with *consistency or change* in that behavior from one occasion to another, for that population of social units.

#7b. Another kind of information comes from correlations between two variables that have the same occasion in common but different behaviors. (Correlations of B_1O_1 with B_2O_1.) These have to do with *convergence* (or lack of convergence) of those behavior measures within each occasion, for that population of social units.

#7c. A third kind of information comes from correlations between two variables that have different behaviors and different occasions. (Correlations of B_1O_1 with B_2O_2.) These cross-correlations have to do with the degree to which one behavior on one occasion *influences* (causes, or predicts) a different behavior on a different occasion, across the social units of that population.

We will hold off on further discussion of the meaning and use of these patterns of relations until the relations of S-B-O array types #8 and #9 have been presented, except to note the following: Correlations of the first subtype (#7a) are about consistency (or change) over time; correlations of the second subtype (#7b) are about convergence (or its lack) among behaviors; and correlations of the third subtype (#7c) are about influence relations (or independence) across both behaviors and occasions.

S-B-O Array #8: Process Patterns
Two or a Few Social Units
and Behaviors, Many Occasions

In S-B-O array #8, the investigator gathers observations about two or a few behaviors for two or a few social units, for a large number of occasions. If the social units are individuals, such a study might be done to compare the temporal patterns of certain behaviors for those persons. If the social units are organizations, the study might involve comparing the trend of monthly rates of each of several production variables for each of several plants. As for type #7, this type of array yields three different sets of correlational information.

#8a. One kind of information comes from correlations (across occasions) between two variables that have the same social unit in common but refer to different behavior variables. (Correlations of S_1B_1 with S_1B_2.) These have to do with a pattern (over occasions) of convergence of those behaviors within the system represented by that social unit.

#8b. Another kind of information comes from correlations between two variables that have the same behavior in common but different social units. (Correlations of S_1B_1 with S_2B_1.) These have to do with patterns (over occasions) of similarity or difference between different social units on that behavior.

#8c. A third type of information comes from correlations between two variables that have different social units and different behaviors. (Correlations of S_1B_1 with S_2B_2.) These have to do with the degree to which one behavior of one social unit is associated with (accompanies) a different behavior of a different social unit, in a patterned way across occasions.

Note, here, that subtype #8a generates relations about *convergence among behaviors,* and subtype #8c generates relations about *influence* across both behavior and social units, but subtype #8b generates relations that are about *similarity* (or difference) *between social units.*

S-B-O Array #9: Behavior Patterns
Two or a Few Social Units
and Occasions, Many Behaviors

In S-B-O array #9, the investigator gathers observations on each of a number of behaviors, for two or a few social units on two or a few occasions. Such a study might have to do with examining the behavior profiles of different individuals on different occasions, to see both inter-individual and intraindividual differences. As for types #7 and #8, this type of S-B-O array yields three different sets of correlational information.

#9a. One kind of information comes from correlations (across the profile of behaviors) between two variables that have reference to the same social unit but are drawn from different occasions. (Correlation of S_1O_1 with S_1O_2.) These have to do with consistency (or change) in a profile of behaviors from one occasion to another, for a given social unit.

#9b. Another kind of information comes from correlations between two variables that are drawn from the same occasion but refer to different social units. (Correlation of S_1O_1 with S_2O_1.) These have to do with similarity (or difference) in behavior profiles between two different social units, on any one occasion.

#9c. A third kind of information comes from correlations between two variables that refer to different social units and are drawn from different occasions. (Correlation of S_1O_1 with S_2O_2.) These have to do with the degree to which the profile of behaviors of a given social unit on a given occasion corresponds to (influences, elicits) the same profile of behaviors of a different social unit on a later occasion.

Note that subtype #9a generates relations about *consistency/change* in the profile of behaviors from one occasion to another; subtype #9b generates relations about *similarity/difference* in the profile of behavior between different social units; and subtype #9c generates relations about *influence* on the profile of behaviors across both social units and occasions.

Research Information in the Three-Way Arrays

Earlier we listed three one-way S-B-O arrays, and indicated the three corresponding patterns of relations that they can yield. Then, we listed three two-way S-B-O arrays, indicated two different ways that each can be used, and identified the six patterns of relations that can be derived from them. In this section, we have listed three ways that a three-way S-B-O array can be constructed, and indicated three kinds of correlations that each such pattern can yield. But we did not discuss the meanings associated with the information that comes from each of those kinds of correlational patterns. We will now discuss the kinds of correlations that come out of the three way arrays, but we will regroup them so that we can make their meanings more explicit.

In that earlier discussion, we identified four types of correlations overall. Some of those types of correlations have to do with *consistency/ change* across occasions (#7a and #9a). Some have to do with *convergence/nonconvergence* between variables (#7b and #8a). Some have to do with *similarity/difference* between social units (#8b and #9b). Finally, the cross-correlations have to do with *influence/independence* across two of the axes (#7c, #8c, and #9c). We will use that grouping to discuss the kinds of research information these correlations contain.

Consistency/Change. Two of the patterns of relations have to do with exploring consistency or change over time. One (#7a) has to do with consistency of a behavior between two occasions, among members of a population of social units. It refers to *behavior consistency (or change) in a population.* The other (#9a) has to do with consistency (or change) of a social unit, from one occasion to another, in its pattern or profile of behaviors. It refers to *system consistency (or change) of a behavior profile.* (System, here, means a particular social unit—person, group, community.)

Convergence/Nonconvergence. Two of the patterns of relations have to do with exploring convergence or lack of it between two or more behavior variables. One of them (#7b) has to do with convergence of two or more behaviors (across members of the population of social units) within a single occasion. It refers to convergence of a behavior pattern within an occasion—a *situational convergence.* It is one of the most common types of research information we gather in our studies. The other one (#8a) has to do with convergence, or lack of it, of two or more behaviors (across a set of occasions) for a given social unit. It refers to a *system behavior pattern.*

Similarity/Difference. Two of the patterns of relations have to do with exploring similarities or differences between two or more social units. One of them (#8b) has to do with similarity of two or more social units (across occasions) on some one behavior. It refers to *behavioral similarity.* The other (#9b) has to do with similarity of two or more social units (across a profile of behaviors) on some one occasion. It refers to *situational similarity.*

Influence/Independence. The final three of the patterns of relations— the three involving cross correlations—all have to do with exploring influence (or independence) that extends across two of the axes of S-B-O. One of them (#7c) has to do with the extent to which one behavior on one occasion is associated (within some population of social units) with a different behavior on a subsequent occasion. Thus, it refers to the *functional interdependence of two behaviors, X then Y.* This, too, is a common pattern of research information in our field. (It can be argued that all studies involving experimental manipulations contain this kind of information: X, then Y, implies at least two variables and two occasions.)

A second influence relation (#8c) has to do with the extent to which one behavior by one social unit is associated with a different behavior by a different social unit, throughout a series of occasions. If the two social units are individuals, we could call this kind of relation *role differentiation*. In a more general language, we can call such relations *specialization of function*.

The third of these influence relations (#9c) has to do with the extent to which the behavior pattern exhibited by a given social unit at one time is exhibited by a different social unit at a subsequent time. If the two social units are individuals (say, older and younger siblings), we might regard this pattern as indicating that one S *modeled* the earlier behavior of the other. In more general terms, we could call it *cross-system modeling*.

Concluding Comments

These nine patterns of relations can be derived from three-axis S-B-O arrays. Some deal with consistency/change across times, some with convergence of behaviors, some with similarity of social units, and some with cross system influence relations. As noted, some of them are related to some of the simpler patterns that can be derived from one-axis and two-axis S-B-O arrays. Together, these nine patterns, plus the nine simpler ones already presented, make up the set of forms of research information that we can derive from a study. All of the studies in our field generate research information that fits one or more of these 18 patterns. Those patterns are shown in Table 5.1.

Of these 18 patterns of relations, 12 are time-related in one or another form. Some of them are time related because they are correlations over occasions. Some of them are time related because they are comparisons between patterns in successive occasions. Only those that involve but a single occasion (types #1, #3, #4a, #4b, #7b, #9b) do not have direct reference to temporal factors such as those discussed earlier in this book. Hence, these S-B-O arrays, and the patterns of research information that they can yield, provide a rich context for considering temporal factors in our studies. The remaining sections of this chapter will explore some of the implications of those temporal patterns.

USING THE S-B-O TEMPLATE TO
TIME-STRUCTURE STUDY PLANS

The S-B-O template provides a generic time-structure for study designs. All (18) of the potential types of relations can yield useful information about the phenomena of the social and behavioral sciences.

TABLE 5.1
Summary of S-B-O Arrays

S-B-O Arrays	Pattern of Relations

One-Axis S-B-O Arrays
  #1:   behavior profiles
          distribution of a set of behaviors on one occasion for a social
          unit
  #2:   temporal profiles
          distribution of a behavior of a social unit over a set of occasions
  #3:   population profiles
          distribution of a behavior in members of a population on a single
          occasion

Two-Axis S-B-O Arrays
  #4:   single occasion
  #4a: stable behavior relations
          several behaviors within a population
  #4b: comparative behavior profiles
          many behaviors for each of several social units
  #5:   single social unit
  #5a: behavior profile change
          many behaviors on several occasions
  #5b: temporal behavior relations
          several behaviors over many occasions
  #6:   single behavior
  #6a: temporal profile comparisons
          several social units for many occasions
  #6b: reliability studies
          a population of social units on several occasions

Three-Axis S-B-O Arrays
  #7:   population patterns
          patterns of a population of social units for several behaviors
          in each of several occasions
  #8:   process patterns
          patterns over a set of occasions for several behaviors for each
          of several social units
  #9:   behavior patterns
          patterns of a population of behaviors for several social units
          on each of several occasions

Types of Relations in the Three-Axis S-B-O Arrays

#7a, #9a:	consistency/change over occasions
#7b, #8a:	congruence/noncongruence among behavior variables
#8b, #9b:	similarity/difference between social units
#7c, #8c, #9c:	influence/independence across two axes

Most of those types of relations bear on temporal issues. This section discusses ways to make more use of the temporal information that is inherent in the occasion axis, and at the same time, relates use of the S-B-O template to several current methodological approaches: auto-correlation, interrupted time-series designs, and cohort designs.

Using the Temporal Information
Inherent in the Occasion Axis:
Auto-Correlation in the S-B-O Template

The S-B-O schema deals with time only as a time-ordered set of occasions. But the occasion axis, by its nature, provides more temporal information than just an order relation. Consider the difference in information that we have when we get a sample of population units, compared to when we get a sample of behavioral variables, and when we get a sample of occasions. Often, with population units, we draw the sample randomly from a known or hypothetical population. Unless we take steps to collect further tag data about each case (e.g., age, sex) at the time we specify the sample, we will know nothing about attributes of the population members nor about their relations to one another. With a sample of behavior variables we are one step better off. We seldom select behavior variables randomly, but select them systematically with respect to their content. This gives us tag information about the qualitative nature of the variables (what kind of behavior it is), but still tells us little about the relations of one behavior variable to another. Often, exploring such relations among behavior variables is the focal purpose of the study.

But when we select a sample of temporal occasions, we automatically know (or easily can know) the time location of each occasion with reference to some external clock. We can use that information to establish both the time order relation and the time interval relation for all pairs of occasions. Even if we were to select observation times randomly, we nevertheless would still know the order relation and interval duration for every pair of sampled occasions.

Frequently, researchers specify two or more kinds of occasions—that is, different kinds of situations—and sample specific occasions from each of them. Doing that adds qualitative information about each occasion. Yet, we still know the order and interval relations, both for every within-situation pair of occasions and for every between-situation pair as well. Thus, we always have the makings of a time-structure for the set of occasions, and that time-structure contains far more intricate information about time relations among the elements than we usually have for either the set of behaviors or the set of social units.

We can make that temporal structure work for us in our explorations of many of the S-B-O data arrays. Specifically, we can construct a number of time scores for each occasion or pair of occasions. First, we can translate the temporal location of each occasion into a score that is its serial position within the set of occasions of the study. From that, we can calculate the order relation between each pair of occasions. We can also use the time-location information to calculate a third score for each pair of occasions: duration of the interval between the pair.

We can calculate that set of three scores for any pair of observations in our S-B-O array. If the two observations are from the same occasion, zero scores will reflect simultaneity between the two observations. Otherwise, the magnitude of the scores will reflect the temporal distance between the pair of observations.

Such time order and interval information can be used in still another way. Some forms of spectral analysis (see discussion, Chapter 4) make use of auto-correlations. These are covariations between: (a) the string of scores of a given behavior variable for a given social unit measured across an ordered series of occasions, and (b) the same string of scores, offset by a lag of one (or two, or any number of) observation units. Such autocorrelations can be computed on scores from any given S for any given B, in any of the S-B-O arrays that use many occasions (types #2, #5a, #6a, #8a, #8b, and #8c). Autocorrelations provide an entrée to analyses that identify cyclical periodicities. In principle we can identify cycles over time in any behavioral process for any social unit. Suppose we were to take a given behavior variable, B, and construct a set of autocorrelations for that B over the string of occasions. If the correlations between scores progressively more distant from one another get progressively smaller, we could interpret that as indicating monotonic change over time. If the correlations fall as they get more distant, then rise again (perhaps repeating that fall and rise more than once), that pattern indicates cyclical change over time. A high and significant autocorrelation of a certain lag, say four occasions apart, may indicate that there is a cyclic process with a period equal to a four-occasion duration. To explore that possibility further, we could look for a similarly high correlation at occasion-distances of 8, 12, and so on. Furthermore, if there is a cycle of period four, there should be a strong *negative* correlation at or near lag two; and there should be negative correlations at lags of 6, 10, and so on. (All of this implies, of course, some relatively regular oscillatory function that is symmetrical on both axes—such as a sine wave—and that is not the only kind of temporal pattern that there is. Less regular patterns are even more difficult to find and confirm.)

Exploring the Temporal Shape of Causal Processes: Interrupted Time-Series Designs as S-B-O Arrays

Time-series designs refer to study plans that call for the measurement of key study variables on each of a series of occasions. (S-B-O arrays of types #2, #5a, #6a, #8a, #8b, and #8c fit this prescription.) The locations of those occasions in time are known in advance to the investigator.

Cook and Campbell (1979) discuss interrupted time-series designs as one form of quasi-experimental design. In interrupted time-series designs, an experimental intervention, X, is interposed between two of a series of successive measurements of other key study variables. Such quasi-experimental designs make it possible to get some inferential leverage about cause/effect relations even in the absence of randomization. Such time-series designs are one form of general data collection strategy that takes a number of time factors into account. In the preceding chapter, we discussed an interrupted time-series format as the basis for study of nonlinear and nonmonotonic change and to detect cycles. (For more extended descriptions and discussion of such designs, see, for example, Box & Jenkins, 1970; Catalano, Dooley, & Jackson, 1983; Cook & Campbell, 1979; Horne, Yang, & Ware, 1982.)

To use time-series designs as a general data collection strategy for taking temporal factors into account, however, requires a great deal of consideration of both the locations in time and the intervals between successive experimental events (treatments and observations), as we have suggested in a number of places earlier in this book. Those intervals ought to be chosen with some reference to hypotheses about causal intervals, and about the temporal shape of the X-Y relations. Often the time intervals between successive measurements, or occasions, are made equal. Unfortunately, this is often done not so much for theoretical reasons but for neatness of the data set and experimental convenience.

Nevertheless, the central ideas involved in the interrupted time-series design can be used in conjunction with our S-B-O template to gain some conceptual leverage in regard to temporal features of the substantive phenomena of our field.

Standard interrupted time-series designs, a la Cook and Campbell (1979), are quasi-experimental arrangements that insert an experimental manipulation (X) at one or more places in an ordered string of measurements or observations (Y's). (As used in earlier chapters of this book, a Y is a measurement or observation of an S-B-O combination—some behavior of some social unit at some time.) Such time-series designs permit the researcher to ask about a change in level of a behavior process, Y, before versus after the occurrence of X; or a change in slope of Y on the time continuum represented by the time series (i.e., the series of occasions), before versus after the occurrence of X. But to do so, the situation and the data must fit several fairly strong conditions.

First, to interpret the meaning of a *level difference* (or lack of such a difference) at the critical interval (from the treatment X to the next subsequent observation, Y) requires at least two sets of observations prior to the manipulation, and at least two sets of observations subsequent to it. To interpret the meaning of a *slope difference* at the critical interval requires at least three sets of observations prior to the manipulation and at least three sets subsequent to it. Either of these also requires:

(1) A causal process (i.e, the effect of X on Y) that does not take any longer than one critical interval (from X to the next observation, Y) to operate.
(2) A causal process that does not wane (very much) for at least 3 intervals (critical interval plus two).
(3) A causal process that is linear or nearly so, or at least monotonic in its operation over time.
(4) The absence of other, nonmonotonic system processes, that affect Y but that are not part of the X-Y causal process under study, for at least two intervals before X, and for at least two intervals after it.

In order to detect cycles in such a time series the periods of the cycles must be: (a) longer than the interval between adjacent sets of observations (Y_i to Y_j); and (b) shorter than half the time from the very first to the very last sets of observations. Cyclic processes with periodicities exactly matching the interval between observations (Y_i to Y_j), or a submultiple of it, could not be noticed in such data. Cyclic processes longer than the Y-Y interval will confound the analysis if they are ignored. Cyclic processes much shorter than the Y-Y interval, and not a submultiple of it, will partially be overlooked and will partially confound the information obtained from these analyses. Even more crucially, for cycles to be detected in such data requires that the investigator be sensitive to the idea that cyclic processes abound!

However, we can take the temporal template we have laid out thus far—the S-B-O template coupled to the idea of time-structuring the set of occasions—as a base for asking stronger questions than are usually asked in such a time series format. Note that all of the correlations in the basic S-B-O template can be based on observations of unmanipulated variables (Ys). But in an interrupted time series quasi-experiment, at least one of the variables is a manipulated condition (an experimental treatment, X). This constrains the set of relations we can study (e.g., we would not ask if Y causes X). But it also strengthens some of the inferences we can make about the X-Y relation over time.

Time Structuring the Population of Social Units: Cohort Designs as Overlayed S-B-O Templates

The term *cohort design* here refers to a set of data collection and comparison strategies designed to help the researcher untangle the naturally confounded influences of: (1) history (or secular trends or true social change), (2) developmental or maturational effects, (3) generational effects (or the interaction of history with a particular stage of development), (4) variation or instability over time of the process variables being studied (which could, of course, reflect cyclical patterns of those processes), and (5) measurement error.

Basically, cohort designs involve a set of planned comparisons built around a systematic set of measures of the behavior variables of interest (several Bs). The set of variables is measured at each of a number of measurement occasions (Os), for all of the members of each of a number of different samples. Each sample is made up of a number of individuals of each of a series of age cohorts. The intervals between measurement occasions are selected so that the measurement periods fall at each of a number of parallel times in the life cycles of the members of each age cohort. The occasions are located in time so that the measurement periods for each cohort, measurement time, and life cycle time fall at different historic (i.e., calendar) times. Such a complex of measurements allows at least partial disentanglement of the historic, maturational, generational, and measurement effects. (For further discussions of these types of designs, and what they can and cannot do, see Adam, 1978; Baltes, 1968; Baltes & Schaie, 1976; Bengtson, Furlong, & Laufer, 1974; Buss, 1973; Horn & Donaldson, 1976; Schaie, 1965.)

For example, suppose that each batch of observations consisted of a set of social units (for ease of discussion, let's assume they are individuals) initially measured on the behavior variables of interest at some particular point in time (e.g., 1960). Suppose that batch of social units contains some members who are 20 years old, some who are 30, some who are 40, and so on, at the time they are observed on that first occasion (1960). Suppose, further, that those same social units (or as many as could be rounded up) were observed again on an occasion exactly five years later, then again after another five years, and another, and so on. Those observations were with respect to the same set of behavior variables (insofar as that is possible to do). Suppose still further that, on that second observation time (1965, year five of the study), an initial set of observations are made on another batch of social units, who are neatly structured in age (at that time) parallel to the first batch when they started. Those observations would be on the same behavior variables. Suppose that, as for the first sample, you followed up that second sample every five years with observations on the same set of behavioral variables. Suppose even further that, at year 10 (1970), you began still a third sample—similarly age structured—with observations every five years on the same set of behavioral variables. Such a set of observations provides a framework for a powerful longitudinal-cross-sectional cohort design.

Suppose we laid out the data from such a set of observations into a matrix with time along the east-west axis, and batches of social units down the north-south axis, and with age-batches nested in an orderly way within each cell—one layer of such a matrix for each behavioral variable. Comparisons along the time axis refer to history, or social change; and of course they are confounded in that form with age (maturation), generational, and cohort effects, and with the reactive effects of repeated measurements of the same social units on the same behavioral variables. We can make some comparisons across cells for the age-structured portions of each batch of cases. With sufficiently complex comparisons, we can tease out the effects of age uncontaminated by history, cohort, and generational effects. (A generational effect, by the way, can be regarded as a history by maturation interaction, or an interaction of history with age at time of certain events.)

Cohort designs represent one kind of time structuring. They have some advantages but also some major limitations. Cohort designs can be thought of as several interlocked and overlayed three-axis S-B-O arrays, or as a multiple sample four dimensional S-B-O array—the fourth dimension being generation, or age at first testing. Generally, cohort designs are better for exploring monotonic/linear changes than for examining cyclical ones. This is the case in part because they usually deal with relatively long periods of time, and consequently use relatively gross intervals between measures. Their scope and complexity make them very expensive to carry out. They do not entirely separate out the confounded factors (see Adam, 1978). Nonetheless, as with autocorrelation, interrupted time-series designs, and the other methodological techniques noted in this and earlier chapters, the underlying ideas of cohort designs can be used in conjunction with our S-B-O template to aid our study of temporal issues.

CONCLUDING COMMENTS

We have argued in this chapter, and indeed throughout this book, that social and behavioral science researchers can increase their ability to gain information about, and hence to come to understand, the phenomena of their field if they plan their studies to take better account of the myriad of temporal factors that infuse the substance of our field. The first three chapters of the book focussed on identifying key temporal issues in the methodology of our field, both at the relatively macrolevels of research strategy and study design, and at the more microlevels of research operations. In the fourth chapter, we discussed a number of techniques that could be of help—at a relatively microlevel— in attempting to take some of these temporal factors into account. There, the focus was on ways to explore temporal as well as logical features of the X-Y causal interval within a given study.

In this final chapter, we have shifted our attention back again to a relatively more macrolevel. We laid out a broad, generic blueprint or template for study planning. That template will let the investigator give much more systematic consideration to many temporal factors than is usually done in study planning in the social and behavioral sciences. That template does not provide a solution to any of the temporal issues raised in earlier chapters of this book. What it does, rather, is to heighten the researcher's consciousness vis-à-vis those temporal factors.

These temporal issues pose serious problems for our ability to continue to advance our knowledge in the social and behavioral sciences. We certainly won't find solutions to these issues until we at least begin to pay attention to them. Thus, we believe, to sensitize researchers in the social and behavioral sciences (including ourselves) to these and other temporal issues is at least a step toward development of a more time-sensitive research methodology for our field.

REFERENCES

Adams, J. (1978). Sequential strategies and the separation of age, cohort, and time-of-measurement contributions to developmental data. *Psychological Bulletin, 85,* 1304-1316.

Baltes, P. B. (1968). Longitudinal and cross-sectional sequences in the study of age and generation effects. *Human Development, 11,* 145-171.

Baltes, P. B., & Schaie, K. W. (1976). On the plasticity of intelligence in adulthood and old age: Where Horn and Donaldson fail. *American Psychologist, 31,* 720-725.

Bengtson, V. L., Furlong, M. J., & Laufer, R. S. (1974). Time, aging, and the continuity of social structure: Themes and issues in generational analysis. *Journal of Social Issues, 30*(2), 1-30.

Birch, D. (1984). A model of fixed activation time scheduling. *Journal of Mathematical Psychology, 28,* 121-159.

Box, G.E.P., & Jenkins, G. M. (1970). *Time series analysis: Forecasting and control.* San Francisco: Holden-Day.

Budescu, D. V. (1984). Tests of lagged dominance in sequential dyadic interaction. *Psychological Bulletin, 96,* 402-414.

Buss, A. R. (1973). An extension of developmental models that separate ontogenic changes and cohort differences. *Psychological Bulletin, 80,* 466-479.

Campbell, D. T., & Fiske, D. W. (1959). Convergent and discriminant validation by the multitrait-multimethod matrix. *Psychological Bulletin, 56,* 81-105.

Campbell, D. T., & Stanley, J. C. (1966). *Experimental and quasi-experimental designs for research.* Chicago: Rand-McNally.

Catalano, R. A., Dooley, D., & Jackson, R. (1983). Selecting a time-series strategy. *Psychological Bulletin, 94,* 506-523.

Cattell, R. B. (1966). Patterns of change: Measurement in relation to state dimension, trait change, lability, and process concepts. In R. B. Cattell (Ed.). *Handbook of multivariate experimental psychology.* Chicago: Rand McNally.

Cook, T. D., & Campbell, D. T. (1979). *Design and analysis of quasi-experiments for field settings.* Chicago: Rand-McNally.

Dabbs, J. (1983). *Fourier analysis and the rhythm of conversation.* (Educational Research Information Clearinghouse [ERIC] Document ED 222 959).

Dillon, W. R., Madden, T. J., & Kumar, A. (1983). Analyzing sequential categorical data on dyadic interaction: A latent structure approach. *Psychological Bulletin, 94,* 564-583.

Einhorn, H. J., & Hogarth, R. M. (1986). Judging probable cause. *Psychological Bulletin, 99,* 3-19.

125

Epstein, S. (1983). A research paradigm for the study of personality and emotions. In M. M. Page (Ed.). *Personality—Current theory and research: 1982 Nebraska Symposium on Motivation.* Lincoln: University of Nebraska Press.

Fiske, D. W. (1982). Convergent-discriminant validation in measurements and research strategies. In D. Brinberg & L. H. Kidder (Eds.), *Forms of validity in research* (pp. 77-92). San Francisco: Jossey-Bass.

Gergen, K. (1973). Social psychology as history. *Journal of Personality and Social Psychology, 26,* 309-320.

Gergen, K. (1985). The social constructionist movement in social psychology. *American Psychologist, 40,* 266-275.

Gottman, J. M. (1979). Detecting cyclicity in social interaction. *Psychological Bulletin, 86,* 338-348.

Hammond, K. R., Harm, R. M., & Grassia, J. (1986). Generalizing over conditions by combining the multitrait-multimethod matrix and the representative design of experiments. *Psychological Bulletin, 100,* 257-269.

Harrison, D. A. (1987). *Event history models for absence data.* Unpublished master's thesis. University of Illinois, Urbana-Champaign.

Hedges, S. M., Jandorf, L., & Stone, A. A. (1985). Meaning of daily mood assessments. *Journal of Personality and Social Psychology, 48,* 428-434.

Hewes, D. E., Planalp, S. K., & Streibel, M. (1980). Analyzing social interaction: Some excruciating models and exhilarating results. *Communication Yearbook, 4,* New Brunswick, NJ: Transaction-International Communication Association.

Horn, J. L., & Donaldson, G. (1976). On the myth of intellectual decline in adulthood. *American Psychologist, 31,* 701-719.

Horne, G. P., Yang, M.C.K., & Ware, W. B. (1982). Time series analysis for single-subject designs. *Psychological Bulletin, 91,* 178-189.

Hovland, C. I. & Weiss, W. (1951). The influence of source credibility on communication effectiveness. *Public Opinion Quarterly, 15,* 635-650.

Humphreys, L. G., & Parsons, C. K. (1979). A simplex process model for describing differences between cross-lagged correlations. *Psychological Bulletin, 86,* 325-334.

Kenny, D. A. (1975). Cross-lagged panel correlation: A test for spuriousness. *Psychological Bulletin, 82,* 887-903.

Kerr, N. L. (1981). Social transition schemes: Charting the group's road to agreement. *Journal of Personality and Social Psychology, 41,* 684-702.

Kraemer, H. C., & Jacklin, C. N. (1979). Statistical analysis of dyadic social behavior. *Psychological Bulletin, 86,* 217-224.

Kulka, R. A. (1982). Monitoring social change via survey replication: Prospects and pitfalls from a replication survey of social roles and mental health. *Journal of Social Issues, 38*(4), 17-38.

Larsen, R. J. (1988). *Analytic strategies in the idiographic-monothetic paradigm: Utilizing time as a facet of data.* Unpublished manuscript. Purdue University, West Lafayette, IN.

Lloyd, G.E.R. (1968). *Aristotle: The growth and structure of his thought.* Cambridge: Cambridge University Press.

Manicas, P. T. & Secord, P. F. (1983). Implications for psychology of the new philosophy of science. *American Psychologist, 38,* 399-413.

McGrath, J. E. (1981). Methodological problems in research on stress. In H. W. Krohne & L. Laux (Eds.). *Achievement, Stress, and Anxiety.* New York: Hemisphere.

McGrath, J. E., & Kelly, J. R. (1986). *Time and human interaction: The social psychology of time.* New York: Guilford.

McGrath, J. E., Martin, J., & Kulka, R. C. (1982). *Judgment calls in research.* Beverly Hills, CA: Sage.

Moore-Ede, M. C., Sulzman, F. M., & Fuller, C. A. (1982). *The clocks that time us.* Cambridge, MA: Harvard University Press.

Pagels, H. R. (1982). *The cosmic code: Quantum physics as the language of nature.* Toronto, Bantam.

Porges, S. W., Bohrer, R. E., Cheung, M. N., Drasgow, F., McCabe, P. M., & Keren, G. (1980). New time-series statistic for detecting rhythmic co-occurrence in the frequency domain: The weighted coherence and its application to psychophysiological research. *Psychological Bulletin, 88,* 580-587.

Runkel, P. J., & McGrath, J. E. (1972). *Studying human behavior.* New York: Holt, Rinehart, & Winston.

Schaie, K. W. (1965). A general model for the study of developmental problems. *Psychological Bulletin, 64,* 92-107.

Stewart, I. N. & Peregoy, P. L. (1983). Catastrophe theory modeling in psychology. *Psychological Bulletin, 94,* 336-362.

Tucker, L. R. (1966). Some mathematical notes on three-mode factor analysis. *Psychometrika, 31,* 279-311.

Wampold, B. E. (1984). Tests of dominance in sequential categorical data. *Psychological Bulletin, 96,* 424-429.

Warner, R. M. (1984). *Rhythm as an organizing principle in social interaction: Evidence of cycles in behavior and physiology.* Unpublished manuscript, University of New Hampshire, Dover.

Warner, R. M., Kenny, D. A., & Stoto, M. (1979). A new round-robin analysis of variance for social interaction data. *Journal of Personality and Social Psychology, 37,* 1742-1757.

Webb, E. J., Campbell, D. T., Schwartz, R. D., Sechrest, L. & Grove, J. B. (1981). *Nonreactive measures in the social sciences* (2nd ed.). Boston, MA: Houghton Mifflin.

GLOSSARY

actors-behaving-in-context. Term used by Runkel and McGrath (1972), to designate a single datum or observation. Actor here means the social unit (individual, group, organization, etc.) whose behavior is being observed. Behavior refers to the property or attribute of the actor's state or action that is observed. Context refers to the physical, social, and temporal setting in which the behavior takes place. (Related terms: S-B-O array; S-B-O template.)

ahistorical (systems) **causality.** A view of causality that holds that cause/effect relations ought to be dealt with in terms of interdependence among contemporaneous forces or factors within a system, rather than as a single chain of action of temporally sequenced conditions. (Compared with causal inferences.)

archival records. Term used by Webb et al. (1981) to refer to research data that is derived from documents, records, and other such material (e.g., production records, newspaper files, speeches, diaries, etc.), that were accumulated initially for administrative or other nonresearch purposes. (Related terms: observations, self-reports, trace measures.)

auto-correlations. Statistical techniques by which a set of scores on a given behavior variable over a series of occasions (for a given social unit) is correlated with "itself" with a lag of 1, or 2, or more occasions. For example, if a set of scores is to be correlated with itself with lag of 1, then correlations are determined by pairing occasion 1 with occasion 2, occasion 2 with occasion 3, and so on. (Related term: spectral analyses.)

behavior variables. Our term for the attributes or properties or contents of a set of observations. (Related terms: "actors-behaving-in-context," occasions, social units, S-B-O array, S-B-O template.)

catastrophe theory. A mathematical theory that deals with systems that have multiple stable states and exhibit discontinuous functions. See Stewart and Peregoy (1983).

causal condition (cause). A variable or condition, X, observed in or imposed upon a situation, and regarded by the investigator as the putative basis for, or force underlying, the occurrence or change of some outcome variable, Y.

Such causal conditions can take any of at least four temporal "shapes": A one-shot agent; a continuing condition; an accumulating condition; a recurrent condition. (Related terms: experimental treatment, independent variable.)

causal inferences (causal relation). Drawing logical conclusions, from a set of empirical evidence, about whether or not the presence and magnitude of a certain observed variable (outcome variable, Y, in the terms used in this book) was brought about or caused by the prior presence and action of a certain other observed or deliberately imposed variable (causal agent X, in the terms used in this book). (Related term: logical-causal order.)

causal process interval. The temporal interval between the occurrence of a putative causal variable, X, and the observation or measurement of the outcome variable, Y. (Related terms: temporal interval; the X-Y interval.)

cause. See causal condition.

circadian rhythms. Endogenous (inherent) rhythmic (cyclic, oscillatory) processes in many species of plants and animals. Under special "free-running" conditions, they show daily periodicities (cycles, rhythms) that are near to but not exactly 24 hours in length. Under usual conditions, they become entrained to (synchronized with) the 24-hour daily rotation of the planet and its accompanying dark/light and temperature cycles. See Moore-Ede et al., (1982). (Related terms: cycles, endogenous rhythms, endogenous system processes, oscillations, periodicities, rhythms.)

cohort designs. A type of complex study design intended to help separate out historical effects, developmental (generational) effects, measurement effects, and their interactions, in the study of social change. A cohort refers to a sample of social units who are at the same developmental stage (age) at the time of their observation. A cohort design requires that samples from a number of different cohorts be observed at each of a series of different times. For further discussion of their strengths and weaknesses see: Adam, (1978); Schaie, (1965). (Related terms: interrupted time-series designs, longitudinal designs, time-series designs.)

computer simulations. A class of research strategies that involve development and use of a computer model of a given (class of) real world systems. All variables in the (model of the) system are represented in ways so that, when the simulation is "run," they show their effects, and the effects of their interactions with other variables, on one or more outcome variables that reflect the operation of that system. For further discussion, see Runkel and McGrath, (1972). (Related terms: experimental simulations, formal theory, other research strategies.)

conceptual time. Our term for the time frame used to represent the operation of system processes within the theory or conceptualization of the system under study. Conceptual time is distinguished from the time frame of real world systems operating under natural conditions (system time or real time), and the time frame imposed on events within an experimental study (experimental time). (Related terms: experimental time, real time or system time, temporal context, temporal scale.)

confounding. A general methodological term used to refer to any of a number of ways in which the effects of variables (sometimes unknown to or hidden from the investigator) may obscure (or falsely enhance) relations between other variables within a set of empirical observations. (Related terms: control, counterbalance, plausible rival hypotheses, validity.)

control. A general methodological term, used in several senses in the context of controlling a variable that is important within a problem under study, but that is not itself part of the study focus. Experimental control of a variable means to hold that variable constant for all cases in a study (e.g., use only male subjects, or have all respondents answer the same questionnaire). Statistical control of a variable means to let the variable vary within the study, but observe its values for each case, and use that set of observations to "statistically remove" its effects on the X-Y relations under study. A variable can also be controlled by counterbalancing—e.g., if groups are going to work on two problems, some groups would work on A, then B, and other groups would work on B, then A. The term control is also used in the context of study design to refer to comparison groups. (Related terms: control group, counterbalance.)

control group. Term used to refer to comparison groups within an experimental design that did not receive some particular experimental treatment, X, (while some other cases, which are to be compared with it, did receive that experimental treatment). (Related terms: control, counterbalance.)

counterbalance. Counterbalance is a general methodological term used to refer to systematic procedures by which sets of experimental events occur in different chronological orders. For example, three different problem solving tasks might be presented to different subsamples in each of the following six orders: A, B, C; A, C, B; B, C, A; B, A, C; C, B, A; C, A, B. Counterbalancing is a way of offsetting ("controlling") the effects of temporal order of the events on the outcome variable(s) Y. (Related terms: control, control group.)

cycle. A cycle is the result of systematic, recurrent variation (oscillation) in presence, direction (i.e., positive or negative), or magnitude of a variable over time. The variable shows a peak (presence, positive value), and a subsequent ebb (absence, negative value) recurrently at some identifiable periodicity (frequency per time interval). For example, a musical tone can be stated as a sound wave with a cycle of a certain frequency. For more discussion of cycles, see Moore-Ede et al. (1982), Warner (1984). (Related terms: oscillation, periodicity, rhythm, sine wave.)

dependent variable. A general methodological term used to refer to variables observed in a research study that are regarded as outcome variables, Y, that are effects, or consequences, or results of operation of some other variable(s) in the situation. (Some of these other variables may be regarded as causal variables). (Related term: independent variable.)

duration. The extent of the temporal interval that characterizes some event. The duration of some event is the time between the beginning of the event and its termination. Duration is to time as length is to space.

endogenous rhythms. Behavioral processes that vary naturally over time in a cyclical pattern—that is, that oscillate at some regular periodicity. (Related terms: cycles, endogenous system processes, oscillations, periodicities, rhythms.)

endogenous system processes. Behavioral processes that are inherent in a given natural system—that is, that do not require any outside source of stimulation to be manifested. Some of those endogenous system processes show endogenous rhythmic patterns. (Related terms: endogenous rhythms, system.)

epochal. A perspective about time that holds that all instants of time are not equivalent and homogeneous, but that certain points in time or periods of time are qualitatively different from one another. For further discussion see McGrath and Kelly (1986). (Related term: phasic.)

experimental simulations. A class of research strategies that involve development and use of a model that represents, in fairly faithful ways, the operation of many portions of a given class of complex natural systems (e.g., an aircraft in flight). Those simulated parts of the system are used in conjunction with the behavior of social units who supply the behavior that completes the system (e.g., an aircraft flight simulator supplies all of the information that a given aircraft in a given kind of flight would provide to a pilot, and responds to pilot control actions in the way that such an aircraft would respond). For further discussion, see Runkel and McGrath, (1972). (Related terms: laboratory experiments, computer simulations, and other research strategies.)

experimental time. The time orders and intervals between experimental events (manipulations and observations) in an experimental study. (Related terms: real time or system time, conceptual time, temporal context, temporal scale.)

experimental treatment. Experimental arrangements by which the investigator deliberately creates certain levels of a given experimental variable, X,—the presumed causal agent(s) the effects of which on an outcome variable, Y, are to be assessed—with different levels of that variable being produced in different subsets of those cases according to experimental plan. (Used synonymously with experimental manipulation). (Related terms: causal condition, independent variable.)

external validity. A general methodological term coined by Campbell and Stanley (1966). It refers to the degree to which the investigator can confidently expect any given set of study results to hold if tested on a different population or on different occasions. Note that internal validity and external validity refer to *relations between two or more variables,* whereas some other uses of validity (as in studies of the validity of a test) refer to *attributes of a single test or measure*. (Related terms: generalization, internal validity, validity.)

fidelity. Term used, especially in relation to computer simulations and experimental simulations, to refer to the degree to which a given simulation closely maps (that is, is faithful to) the states and processes of the natural systems to which the simulation is intended to refer.

field experiments. A class of research strategies in which the investigator intervenes by manipulating one major variable in the otherwise naturally occurring situation. (Related terms: field studies and other research strategies.)

field studies. A class of research strategies that involve making observations in a naturally occurring situation while disturbing the naturalness of that situation as little as possible. (Related terms: field experiments, and other research strategies.)

formal theories. A class of research strategies that involve generating conceptual formulations that systematically state, make hypotheses about, and interpret the problem/system under study. (Related terms: computer simulations and other research strategies.)

frequency. A term used in general to refer to number of some kind of event per time unit; and a term used in relation to temporal cycles, to refer to number of oscillations or repetitions of the cycle per time unit. (Related terms: cycle, oscillation, periodicity, rate, rhythm, sine wave.)

galvanic skin response (GSR). A putative measure of stress, which is based on measurement of the conductivity of the skin. Skin conductivity varies as a function of activity of sweat glands. The GSR assumes that increased activity of the sweat glands, hence increased skin conductivity, represents increased stress.

generalization. A general methodological term used to refer to the degree to which a set of findings can be expected to hold if the same research questions are asked again, for different actors, behaviors, contexts. (Related terms: external validity, standardization.)

hazard rate models. A class of mathematical models, particularly useful for analyzing low base rate events, which model changes in system states. For more discussion see: Birch, (1984); Harrison, (1987).

history. A general methodological term popularized by Campbell and Stanley (1966) as one of seven major classes of plausible rival hypotheses or threats to the internal validity of a study finding. The term history is used to refer to any condition external to the actor that might occur between prior and subsequent measures of an outcome variable (Y), or between occurrence of an experimental condition (X) and a subsequent measure of an outcome variable (Y), other than those intended as part of an experimental situation, that might have produced or affected the subsequent level of Y. History refers to unintended effects occurring in time, not to time itself. (Related terms: internal validity, plausible rival hypotheses.)

independent variable. Independent variable is a general term in the research methodology of the social and behavioral sciences. It is used to refer to variables observed in, or especially those imposed on, a research study that are regarded as causal variables that are expected to produce effects, or consequences, on an outcome variable, Y. (Related terms: causal condition, dependent variable, experimental treatment.)

instrument change. A general methodological term popularized by Campbell and Stanley (1966) as one of seven major classes of plausible rival hypotheses or threats to the internal validity of a study finding. Their original term for this threat was *instrument decay;* instrument change is more general. The term is used to refer to all of the ways in which a given measuring instrument may become modified over time and with additional use. For physical measuring instruments these ways include such factors as breakage, rust, shifts in calibration. For human observers, these ways include such factors as learning, fatigue, shifts in motivation of the observer. (Related terms: internal validity; rival plausible hypotheses.)

interaction. The term interaction is used in two unrelated ways in the social and behavioral sciences. In its statistical usage, which is the main one drawn upon in the text of this book, the term interaction refers to the *joint* effect of two or more causal factors, Xs, on some outcome variable(s), Y, over and above what the additive effects of each of the two Xs, acting separately, would have been. In its substantive use, which we draw upon in our examples of group interaction process, the term interaction refers to the process by which two or more people carry out common tasks or otherwise behave in an interdependent way in relation to one another and to their common surroundings.

internal validity. A general methodological term coined by Campbell and Stanley (1966). It refers to the degree to which—when empirical results of a study show a relation between an imposed causal condition, X, and an outcome variable of interest, Y—the investigator can confidently conclude that X probably caused Y. Note that internal validity and external validity refer to *relations between two or more variables,* whereas some other uses of validity (such as validity of a particular test) refer to *attributes of a single test or measure.* (Related terms: external validity, plausible rival hypotheses, validity.)

interrupted time-series designs. A class of study designs, described by Campbell and Stanley (1966) as a type of *quasi-experimental* design, in which one or more experimental treatments is inserted within a time ordered series of measurements of a given set of behavior variables, with the intention of allowing causal inferences based on differences in the shape of the series of measurements before, compared to the series of measurements after, that experimental event. (Related terms: quasi-experiments, time-series designs.)

judgment studies. A class of research strategies that involves having respondents make a series of judgments under systematically varied conditions of judgment or of stimuli, in order to estimate quantitative values of features of the judged stimuli. For more discussion see Runkel and McGrath (1972). (Related terms: sample surveys, other research strategies.)

laboratory experiments. A class of research strategies that involves having experimental participants take part in a concocted situation in which the investigator has taken steps to manipulate one or more conditions (experimental treatments, X), and will measure one or more behavior variables (outcome variables, Y) while attempting to control as many other variables as possible. For more discussion, see Runkel and McGrath (1972). (Related terms: experimental simulations, judgment studies, and other research strategies.)

linear, monotonic, and nonmonotonic functions of time. The term linear has several different meanings. In the context of this book, the term linear is used most often to refer to a particular form of the function (relation) between a variable and a measure of time. A positive linear relation of a variable with time means that for each equal increment of time there is an equal increment of that variable. Thus, for a linear relation, the variable increases evenly and continuously with the passage of time, *without limit.* Variables that show a decreasing amount of increase with the passage of more and more units of time (sometimes called a diminishing returns function), or that show an increasing amount of increase with the passage of more and more time, are said to be monotonic but not linear functions of time. They continue to increase, but not at a uniform rate. Variables that show an increase at first, and later a decrease, with the passage of time—or vice versa—are said to be nonmonotonic.

logical-causal order. A general methodological term referring to the assumption, within the scientific paradigm, that causal factors lead to or generate effects, hence that the former logically (as well as chronologically) precede the latter, with or without intervening processes that mediate the relation. (Related term: temporal order.)

longitudinal designs. A general methodological term referring to a class of research designs in which a given set of behavior variables are observed for the same members of a given population (a set of social units, in the terms of this book) on each of at least two occasions separated in time. The term usually refers to studies in which there are multiple waves of observations, or the time from first to final wave of observations is a substantial calendar time—months or years. (Related terms: cohort designs, time-series designs.)

Markov chain models. A class of mathematical models that deal with systems of probabilistic relations (as distinct from deterministic ones), and operate by tracing the probabilities of transitions from given states of the system to any given subsequent state. The subclass of those models most frequently used in the social and behavioral sciences are those that deal only with single links, and that make two important assumptions: That the probabilities associated with transitions from one particular state to another are the same at different points in time (stationarity), and that the factors affecting the transition from a given state to another are not effected by prior states (path independence). (Related terms: path independence, stationarity, stochastic models.)

maturation. A general methodological term popularized by Campbell and Stanley (1966) as one of seven major classes of plausible rival hypotheses or threats to the internal validity of a study finding. Maturation effects refer to the effects on some outcome variable, Y, that can arise because of developmental changes in the social units the behavior of which is being observed. (Related terms: internal validity, plausible rival hypotheses.)

measurement. A general methodological term referring to any set of operations by which the level or value or condition of a given attribute is assessed for each of a sample of "cases"—a series of actors-behaving-in-context. The term *observation* is, generally, a synonym. But measurement carries the connotation of a quantitative assessment whereas observation does not. And observation carries the connotation that the evidence is obtained by direct visual search, whereas measurement does not necessarily carry this connotation. (Related terms: observation, measurement error.)

measurement error. A general methodological term, reflecting the assumption that all methods of measurement—observation—are fallible, even when all identifiable sources of systematic error are taken into account. Error of measurement is usually assumed to be *random;* that is, it is assumed that the direction and amount of such error in any given measurement is *independent of the "true" value of the measured behavior.* Hence, measurement error functions much like *noise* does in an acoustic system. (Related terms: measurement, regression to the mean.)

modeling. There are two unrelated uses of this term in the social and behavioral sciences. In its methodological usage, modeling refers to the generation and use of conceptual formulations, usually mathematical ones, which are intended to represent (symbolically) the major variables and interactions among variables of some class of real systems. In that usage, we refer to mathematical models, and to the use of such techniques for *modeling* some class of events or phenomena. (Related terms: computer simulations; Markov chain models; stochastic models). In its substantive use (which is the usage of Chapter 5 of this book), modeling is a term borrowed from social learning theory, which refers to the situation in which one person appears to observe and then to recreate (that is, to imitate) a complex chain of behaviors performed by someone else.

monotonic. See linear, monotonic, and nonmonotonic functions of time.

mortality. A general methodological term popularized by Campbell and Stanley (1966) as one of seven major classes of plausible rival hypotheses or threats to the internal validity of a study finding. Mortality effects refer to potential differences in outcome variable, Y, that can arise because some social units drop out of the study between initial assignment of cases to conditions (that is, to levels or categories of the causal factor, X), and subsequent measurement of the outcome variable, Y. (Related terms: internal validity; plausible rival hypotheses.)

nonmonotonic. See linear, monotonic, and nonmonotonic functions of time.

observation (observational measures). A general methodological term used in two related ways. In one usage, it refers to any set of operations by which the level or value or condition of a given attribute is assessed for each of a sample of "cases"—a series of actors-behaving-in-context. The term *measurement* is, generally, a synonym. But measurement carries the connotation of a quantitative assessment whereas observation does not. In other usage, observation refers to evidence obtained by direct visual search (whereas measurement may be less direct and less visual). (Related terms: archival measures, measurement, self-reports, trace measures.)

occasions. Our term for the points in time at which the waves of observations are made for an array of observations within an S-B-O template. This is our term, within the S-B-O, for the "context" term of Runkel and McGrath's (1972) specification of a basic datum as "actors-behaving-in-context." It is understood that those occasions subsume the situation or setting, as well as the temporal context, within which the observed behavior is taking place. (Related terms: behavior variable, social units, S-B-O arrays, S-B-O template.)

oscillations. A general methodological term referring to variations in state of a system or a process over time. It is generally used to refer to variations that are alternations of on/off or plus/minus states, rather than to variations in processes that are changes in magnitude. (Related terms: cycle, frequency, periodicity, rhythm, sine wave.)

path independence. An assumption made within some mathematical models, notably one-link Markov chain stochastic models. The path independence assumption holds the probability of transition from a given state to any other state is not affected by prior states of that system. (Related terms: Markov chain models, stationarity, stochastic models.)

periodicity. A general methodological term referring to the *rate* of recurrence, or the length of time between occurrences of, oscillations or variations in the state of a system or a process. (Related terms: cycle, frequency, oscillation, rate, rhythm, sine wave.)

phasic. A view of time that holds that the passage of time is not always a smooth flow of homogeneous "units" of time, all identical; rather it can involve a nonuniform flow of units of time that are qualitatively different from one another. See epochal. For further discussion see McGrath and Kelly, 1986. (Related term: epochal.)

phenomena. A term referring to the substantive features or processes, or to the observable events or conditions, within some real world system. It is often used to refer to a recurrent pattern of such features or events, rather than just to a single occurrence.

plausible rival hypotheses. A general methodological term popularized by Campbell and Stanley (1966). A plausible rival hypothesis is any hypothesis other than the one being investigated by the researcher that logically could account for study outcomes and the plausibility of which cannot be ruled out on either logical or empirical bases in that study. Campbell and Stanley identified seven major classes of such plausible rival hypotheses or threats to the internal validity of a study finding. (Related terms: history, instrument change, internal validity, maturation, mortality, reactivity, regression to the mean, selection, testing.)

positivistic paradigm. A paradigm refers to a modus operandi, or general philosophy and strategy for the conduct of science. Positivism refers to the paradigm that has guided research in the social and behavioral sciences for the past century. Positivism, or empiricism, is built on the philosophies of Bacon, Hume, and others, and was popularized within the social and behavioral sciences by Auguste Comte, John Watson, and others. A radical form of that view holds that induction from empirical observations by "objective" (hence replicable) methods of observation, is the only basis for developing scientific knowledge in which we can have confidence. Logical positivism or logical empiricism (or the "hypothetico-deductive method," as it is sometimes referred to in psychology) was a revision of radical empiricism that integrated both inductive and deductive methods. It holds that knowledge accumulates by an iterative process involving theoretical hypotheses derived from prior empirical observations, which are tested and confirmed or disconfirmed by further empirical observations. (For further discussion, and some critique of positivistic views, see Gergen, 1985; Manicas & Secord, 1983.)

priming. A term used in social cognition research. It refers to experimental arrangements in which respondents are exposed to stimuli that are thought to be sensitive to them to certain ideas or emotions (i.e., prime them, as in priming a pump); and that priming is expected to affect their responses to information presented later on, on the outcome variables, Y, that are of interest to the investigator. Note that priming is very similar in form to reactivity or testing effects, one of the classes of plausible rival hypotheses. When considered as a theoretical concept, priming is regarded as the basis for substantive conclusions. When viewed as a methodological artifact, reactivity or testing effects are regarded as threats to the internal validity of findings. (Related terms: plausible rival hypotheses, reactivity effects.)

quasi-experiment. A term popularized by Campbell and Stanley (1966), referring to a class of study design that does not meet one or more of the necessary conditions for a true experiment (usually, because it does not provide randomized allocation to comparison groups), yet is designed in such a way that the investigator can make some causal inferences with some degree of confidence (that is, can rule out some, though not all, of the classes of plausible rival hypotheses). (Related terms: interrupted time-series designs, plausible rival hypotheses, randomization, true experiment.)

randomization. A general methodological term. Randomization, or random allocation of cases to conditions, refers to study procedures by which members of a population of cases (that is, observations of actors-behaving-in-context) that are to be included in a study are allocated to various experimental and comparison conditions so that each has an equal chance of being in each of the conditions. Note that the process of assignment of cases is a random one; there is no guarantee about the nature of the resulting sample of cases in each condition. Note, also, that such random allocation of cases to conditions within a study does not speak to the question of whether random sampling was used in the selection of cases, from some larger population of potential cases, for inclusion in the study. Campbell and Stanley (1966) argue that randomization is one of several necessary conditions for a "true experiment," and that its absence makes a study a "quasi-experiment" or a "preexperimental design." (Related terms: quasi-experiment, true experiment.)

rate. A general methodological term. A rate is the ratio of the frequency of some event per unit of time. (Related terms: frequency, periodicity.)

reaction times. A general methodological term referring to scores that are the time intervals between the onset of some stimulus, instruction, or condition, and the subsequent reaction or response of a social unit to it. (Used synonymously with response latencies.)

reactivity. A general methodological term, related to the term, testing effects, that was popularized by Campbell and Stanley (1966) as one of seven major classes of plausible rival hypotheses or threats to the internal validity of a study finding. Both reactivity and testing effects refer to artifactual effects of some experimental event on an outcome variable, Y, measured subsequent to that experimental event. Testing effects are those effects on Y that arise because of an earlier measurement of that same variable, Y. Reactivity effects include these, but also include effects arising from an earlier experimental treatment, X, or from an earlier measurement of some other variable. Reactivity effects (including testing effects) are effects that arise not because of the putative causal process (the impact of the "active ingredient" of X acting on Y), but as an artifact of the experience of that earlier event. The effect is considered to be potentially an artifact if it seems likely that the prior event sensitized participants to the investigator's (ostensive) interest in some features of the outcome variable, Y, to which participants would otherwise not have been attentive (and to which participants who did not experience the earlier experimental event would not have reacted with changes in Y). (Related terms: plausible rival hypotheses, priming, testing effects.)

realism. A general methodological term referring to one of several conflicting desiderata of research strategies. Realism refers to the degree to which the context or setting in which a given set of observations are made is, or is like, the context or setting that would occur naturally for those social units (actors-behaving-in-context) were there no research study involved. Investigators conducting field studies and studies using related research strategies attempt to maximize realism by disturbing the natural setting of the system under study as little as possible. Investigators conducting laboratory experiments and studies using related research strategies often must sacrifice realism (in the interest in control of measurement and manipulation of variables). Certain research strategies (e.g., field experiments, experimental simulations) are attempts to compromise between realism and control. (Related terms: real time, temporal context.)

real time. Our term for the time frame of the operation of system processes as they occur naturally, without experimental intervention. (Used synonymously with system time). (Related terms: conceptual time, experimental time, temporal context, temporal scale.)

regression to the mean. A general methodological term popularized by Campbell and Stanley (1963) as one of seven major classes of plausible rival hypotheses or threats to the internal validity of a study finding. Regression to the mean refers to a property of all measures (because of measurement fallibility) that extreme scores on an initial measurement of a variable will shift, on the average, toward the 'mean on a later measure of that same variable. (Related terms: internal validity; measurement error; plausible rival hypotheses.)

reliability of measures. A general methodological term referring to the degree to which two or more applications of a measure (or a comparable one) on the same population of cases (or a comparable one) at the same time (or a comparable one), will show the same results. (Related terms: measurement error, reactivity, testing effects.)

research strategy. Term used by Runkel and McGrath (1972), to refer to various kinds of research studies or various classes of setting within which research studies can be carried out. Runkel and McGrath identified (and we deal in this book with) eight such classes of research strategies. (Related terms: field studies, field experiments, experimental simulations, laboratory experiments, judgment studies, sample surveys, formal theories, and computer simulations.)

response latencies. See reaction times.

rhythm. A general methodological term referring to a recurrence, at predictable times (i.e., at some periodicity), of a signal or event or condition or response. (Related terms: circadian rhythm, cycle, frequency, oscillation, periodicity, sine wave.)

sample surveys. A class of research strategies that involves obtaining responses to a series of questions from each member of a sample of some population to which the investigator wishes to extrapolate results of the study, with that sample being selected carefully by procedures that involve a random selection component. (Related terms: judgment study, other research strategies.)

S-B-O array. Our term for a set of observations referring to one or more behavior variables (B) measured on each of one or more social units (S) on each of one or more occasions (O). (Related terms: actors-behaving-in-context, S-B-O template.)

S-B-O template. Our term for a study planning schema that can help the investigator give systematic consideration to a number of factors, especially temporal factors, that are potentially a part of the operation of the system under study. It deals with each of a number of data patterns, or S-B-O arrays, and the research information that can be derived from them. (Related terms: actors-behaving-in-context, S-B-O array.)

selection. A general methodological term popularized by Campbell and Stanley (1966) as one of seven major classes of plausible rival hypotheses or threats to the internal validity of a study finding. Selection refers to study procedures by which cases are allocated to study conditions on any basis other than randomization, especially procedures in which comparison conditions are created by selecting subsets of cases from each of two extremes (or two qualitatively distinct categories) of some condition (e.g., males versus females; infants versus adults; second graders versus seventh graders). Such methods of assigning cases to conditions threaten the internal validity of results of a study because they do not help the investigator reduce or eliminate the plausible rival hypothesis that groups differed before the experimental treatment in some respects other than the intended comparison factor (e.g., gender, or age, in the examples). (Related terms: internal validity, regression to the mean, other plausible rival hypotheses.)

self-report measures. Term used by Webb et al. (1981) to refer to research data that is derived from direct and deliberate responses by study participants (e.g., responses to questionnaires, rating scales, interview questions). (Related terms: archival measures, observational measures, trace measures.)

simultaneity (and succession). A general methodological term referring to the occurrence of two or more denotable events at exactly the same point in time, as distinguished from succession, which refers to the occurrence of two or more events in a denotable temporal order. Whether two events are simultaneous or successive depends, in part, on the degree of temporal refinement of the scale used in making the observations. (Related terms: succession, synchronization.)

sine wave (sinusoidal function). A general methodological term used to refer to a certain class of mathematical functions, or relations between some variable and a time variable. Sine waves are smooth, cyclical functions, that are regular or symmetrical on both axes (that is, there is equal distance between peaks and between troughs, or a regular periodicity, and the amplitude about the midline is symmetrical up and down and is regular from one cycle to another). (Related terms: cycle, frequency, oscillation, periodicity, rhythm.)

social units. Our term for the entities the behavior of which is the focus of sets of observations. This is our term, within the S-B-O, for the "actors" term of Runkel and McGrath's (1972) specification of a basic datum as "actors-behaving-in-context." (Related terms: "actors-behaving-in-context," behavior variables, occasions, S-B-O arrays, S-B-O template.)

spectral analyses (Fourier analyses). A class of mathematical and statistical techniques designed to identify and isolate temporal regularities (i.e., cycles), at each of a number of different periodicities, within a string of time-ordered scores. (Related terms: autocorrelation, time-series design.)

standardization. A general methodological term referring to one of several conflicting desiderata for research study procedures, namely, the attempt to make a number of features of study design and procedures "exactly the same" for all of the cases (all of the observations in the S-B-O array). Standardization is another way to talk about one form of control of variables within a study. (Related terms: control, generalization.)

stationarity. An assumption made within some mathematical models, notably one-link Markov chain stochastic models. The stationarity assumption is that transition probabilities remain the same over time—that is, that the probability of a system moving from one particular state to another is the same throughout that system's history. (Related terms: Markov chain models, path independence, stochastic models.)

stochastic models. A class of mathematical models that deal with systems of relations involving probabilistic relations (as distinct from deterministic ones). The subclass of these most often used in social and behavioral sciences are the Markov chain models that operate by tracing the probabilities of transitions from given states of the system to any given subsequent state. The subclass of those Markov models most frequently used in the social and behavioral sciences are those that deal only with single links, and which make two important assumptions: That the probabilities associated with transitions from one particular state to another are the same at different points in time (stationarity), and that the factors affecting the transition from a given state to another are not effected by prior states (path independence). (Related terms: Markov chain models, path independence, stationarity.)

study design. A general methodological term referring to the plan for conduct of a study and for analysis of study results. Research design and experimental design are used as synonyms, except that research design sometimes refers to the process of study planning, and experimental design implies that the study is a true experiment or at least involves an experimental treatment of one or more variables. (Related terms: experimental treatment, research strategies, true experiment.)

succession. See simultaneity.

synchronization (temporal coordination). A term used with either of two meanings. In one use, synchronization is equivalent to simultaneity. In the other use, it refers to the occurrence of two or more sets of events in functional interdependence or in *temporal coordination* with one another—but not necessarily in a second-by-second simultaneity of actions. (Related terms: simultaneity, succession.)

system. A general term in the research methodology of the social and behavioral sciences. It refers to an integral (functionally interdependent) portion of a context that involves a set of interrelated parts, relations, and processes, and that is in some form of dynamic interaction with its surround. Some system perspectives contain an assumption that there are preferred states of the system to which the system tends (system equilibrium), and that when the system is perturbed out of such a state by some external force, system processes will operate interdependently to reestablish system equilibrium. For further discussion of systems and related concepts, see Runkel and McGrath (1972). (Related term: endogenous system processes.)

system time. Our term for the time frame of the operation of system processes as they occur naturally, without experimental intervention. (Used synonymously with real time). (Related terms: conceptual time, experimental time, time scale.

temporal context. Our term for the temporal part of the overall context, within which system components and processes are embedded. The temporal context is represented by the O, or occasion, axis of our S-B-O template. (Related terms: generalization, realism.)

temporal contiguity and temporal continuity. These terms refer to the *preference,* in most views of causality, for attributing causal status to factors that are close in time to the outcome variables that they affect; and the *requirement,* in those views of causality, that causes must be temporally *connected* to or have temporal continuity with their effects, perhaps by means of a series of mediating processes.

temporal continuity. See temporal contiguity.

temporal interval. Our term to call attention to the temporal, as distinct from the logical-causal, nature of the interval between the occurrence of a causal factor, X, and the observation of an outcome variable of interest, Y. (Related terms: causal process interval, X-Y interval.)

temporal order. Our term to call attention to the temporal, as distinct from the logical-causal, aspect of the order relation between a putative causal factor, X, and an outcome variable of interest, Y. (Related term: logical-causal order).

temporal scale. Our term for the relation between different representations of time orders and intervals among system events, in actual systems, in theories about those systems, and in empirical studies of those systems. System processes under natural conditions (i.e., undisturbed by research activities) unfold in *real time* or *system time;* research studies often impose a quickened *experimental time* on system processes. Symbolic representations of these processes in theories or simulations must interrelate these two times in a conceptual time. (Related terms: conceptual time, experimental time, real time or system time.)

temporal shape. Our term for the form of function (relation) between a variable representing a particular process and a time dimension. We use the term to refer to the functional form of relation of causal variables (experimental treatment X) and an outcome variable, Y, over time. (Related terms: causal process interval, X-Y interval).

temporal window. Our term to draw attention to the importance of the duration of the X-Y interval, that is, the interval between occurrence of putative causal factor, X, and observation of outcome variable, Y. That temporal window is not only the locus of action of the putative causal processes, but also the locus of action of a number of factors that could potentially confound results. (Related terms: confounding, plausible rival hypotheses, X-Y interval.)

testing effects. A general methodological term popularized by Campbell and Stanley (1966) as one of seven major classes of plausible rival hypotheses or threats to the internal validity of a study finding. It is one special form of reactivity. Testing effects refer to the effects of a prior measurement of Y on a later score on that same variable, Y, independent of other factors such as the experimental treatment, X. (Related terms: internal validity, plausible rival hypotheses, reactivity.)

time-series designs. See interrupted time-series designs.

trace measures. Term used by Webb et al. (1981) to refer to measures of accretions or erosions that resulted from aggregate prior behavior. For example, differential wear on museum tiles can be regarded as an index of popularity of different exhibits. The respondent does not know results of his or her behavior is to be used for research purposes (hence, many forms of reactivity are far less likely to occur). But they cannot be attributed either to specific behaviors or to behaviors by specific social units. (Related terms: archival records, observational measures, self-report measures.)

true experiment. A general methodological term popularized by Campbell and Stanley (1966). A true experiment is a study in which: (a) sets of social units from a common population are assigned to experimental and control or comparison conditions by a random allocation procedure; (b) one or more variables (to be regarded as causal factors, X) are deliberately manipulated as experimental treatments in the experimental conditions; and subsequently, (c) one or more outcome variables, Y, are measured, by comparable procedures, for all cases in both experimental and comparison conditions. A true experiment allows the investigator to reduce the plausibility of a number of rival hypotheses on logical grounds. (Related terms: control, control group, quasi-experiment, randomization, study design.)

validity. A general methodological term with many meanings: the degree to which scores on a given behavior variable are to be accepted, with confidence, as measuring the intended construct; the degree to which we can have confidence that an obtained relation between X and Y implies that X caused Y (internal validity), and is likely to recur if the study were repeated (external validity). (Related terms: external validity, internal validity.)

X-Y interval. See causal process interval.

INDEX

ABOUT THE AUTHORS

JANICE R. KELLY is Assistant Professor in the Department of Psychological Sciences at Purdue University. She received her Ph.D. from the University of Illinois, Urbana, in 1987. She is coauthor of another book with Joseph E. McGrath: *Time and Human Interaction* (1986, Guilford Press). Her interests include the social psychology of time, temporal patterns in group performance and interaction, and the effects of mood states on dyadic interaction.

JOSEPH E. McGRATH is Professor of Psychology at the University of Illinois, Urbana. He received his Ph.D. in social psychology from the University of Michigan in 1955. His research interests include small group processes, social and psychological factors in stress, research methodology, and the social psychology of time.

NOTES